The Joy Of

NOT

Knowing
It All

Profiting From Creativity At Work Or Play

Ernie J. Zelinski

VIP BOOKS
Login Publishers Consortium
Chicago, Illinois

VIP BOOKS Edition

Published by:
Visions International Publishing
Edmonton, Alberta, Canada

Distributed to USA bookstores by:
Login Publishers Consortium, Chicago, Illinois
Telephone (312) 733-8228, Fax (312) 733-3107

94 95 96 97 98 99 PS/RRD 10 9 8 7 6 5 4 3 2

Cover design and illustrations by Vern Busby

Direct any inquiries to:

Ernie J. Zelinski   Telephone (403) 436-1798
Box 4072, Edmonton, Alberta, Canada, T6E 4S8

Publisher's Cataloging in Publication
(Prepared by Quality Books Inc.)

Zelinski, Ernie J.

The joy of NOT knowing it all: profiting from creativity at work or play / by Ernie J. Zelinski -- 1st ed.
p. cm.
ISBN 0-9694194-2-2

1. Creative ability. 2. Self-actualization (Psychology) I. Title .

BF408.Z45 1994   153.3'5
QBI94-1489

To all the creative people throughout the ages who have been willing to risk, be different, challenge the status quo, ruffle a few feathers, and in the process, truly make a big difference in this world.

Acknowledgments

I would like to acknowledge the following individuals for being kind and adventurous enough in volunteering to read the manuscript. Besides having spotted spelling and grammatical errors, they offered valuable advice and a great deal of encouragement. All suggestions were very much appreciated.

To all of these individuals, I express a great big thank you. Now it's up to you, the reader, to read on and see if their efforts, along with mine, were worth it.

Forrest Bard
Harvey Deutschendorf
Christopher Cavanaugh
Liz Sherman
Adrianna Iozzo
Stephanie Sharpe
Cindy Lang
Kurian Tharakan
Ross Bradford
Dan O'Brien

Table Of Contents

Preface - The Paradox Of Creativity

A resource vital to modern day business and personal success remains largely unused by the majority of us. This resource is more powerful and plentiful than financial reserves, physical assets, supportive friends, and loyal customers. The resource is our personal creativity; it is a renewable resource and does not cost much to develop. If used properly, our creativity can become our most important asset for achieving personal success.

Creativity is a resource we all possess; however, few of us use it well. The reasons are many: Some of us are unaware of the power of creativity. Some of us are aware of it, but do not know how to use it. Some of us use our creativity but not as often as we should. Some of us are afraid to use it. Only a small minority of us have come close to tapping this personal skill for its full benefits.

> *"Beware when the great God lets loose a thinker on this planet."*
>
> *- Ralph Waldo Emerson*

This book is about how to enhance your creativity. How do I know that your creativity has to be enhanced? I don't. However, I have made a few interesting observations over the last few years while teaching creativity. A strange paradox is evident; the people and organizations who most need to have their creative abilities enhanced are the most resistant to participating in any related learning activities.

The opposite is true with creative people and innovative companies. They are most eager to look at new ways and not-so-new ways to stimulate their creativity. A good example is Grant Lovig and his staff at Company's Coming Publishing. They helped Grant's mother, Jean Pare, market over 8,000,000 of her "Company's Coming" cookbooks in a Canadian industry where 5,000 copies is considered a best-seller. With their phenomenal success in innovative marketing, the staff at Company's Coming are one of the last groups I know which need a lesson in creativity and innovation. Nevertheless, Grant and his staff were most receptive to a creativity seminar which I conducted for them. Many people and companies need to know more about how to be more innovative. They could benefit immensely from improving their creative thinking. There is a Catch-22; because they don't understand the benefits of creativity, they will never take steps to learn about it. Of course, they will never understand the benefits until they take steps to learn about it.

> *"Nothing is more dangerous than an idea when it's the only one you have."*
>
> *- Emile Chartier, Philosopher*

Why do the highly creative individuals of this world spend time on enhancing their creativity? The enhancement of creativity is like most self-improvement activities. Self-improvement is not a destination; it is a journey. Even creative people in this world have to practice and remind themselves what makes people creative and successful. The thing that separates successful people from the less successful ones is that the successful people are always taking part in interesting journeys of learning. They are doers. They continually strive for self-improvement. The less successful are not doers. They may be interested in destinations but resist making the necessary journeys. Without journeys come no new destinations.

The journey of learning helps us get to new and exciting places. My wish is that all participants in my seminars and readers of my books find themselves on a worthwhile journey like the wonderful one I have had in learning about creativity and teaching it to others. Bon voyage.

Ernie J. Zelinski

Introduction To Creativity And Innovation

So What's The Point Of Being Creative?

Hopefully this book will open up a new way of life for you rather than just give you a technique or two to add to those you already use. If you are determined about experiencing the joy of not knowing it all and applying creativity to your work and play, your life will change immensely no matter what your occupation.

In my seminar presentations to professional associations I often say: "A creative businessperson is an entrepreneur, a creative speaker is an orator, a creative welder is a sculptor, a creative engineer is an inventor, and a creative accountant is ... well I guess a creative accountant is an embezzler." Of course I am only kidding. Accountants don't have to be embezzlers to be creative. Even accountants who have rigid guidelines to abide by in their pure accounting work still have much opportunity to be creative in many other aspects of their everyday work.

> *"What's the use of being a genius if you can't use it as an excuse for being unemployed?"*
>
> *- George Barzan*

The same applies to you. Whether you are a nurse, school teacher, janitor, clerical worker, homemaker, manager, truck driver, or bartender, you can find areas in your work in which you can be more creative. Note, if you are employed in an area such as advertising, you are fooling yourself if you think everyone in your field is naturally creative and can't benefit from creativity training. In my seminars several people in advertising have commented how uncreative many people in their field are, and recently The Toronto Star published an article about the lack of creativity in advertising.

You can also profit from creativity at play. Being creative is much more important for handling leisure activities than is having lots of money. I must warn you that if you haven't developed the ability to be creative in your leisure time by the time you retire, you will feel the life of leisure is the biggest rip-off since the last time you got conned into buying the Brooklyn Bridge or swampland in Florida.

If you don't think you have to be creative to succeed in today's world, THINK AGAIN - AND AGAIN - AND AGAIN. (I am just trying to get your mind all revved up for what's ahead.) The most successful people in the 1990s and beyond will be highly creative people who are flexible thinkers and can deal with rapid change.

More and more businesspeople and government leaders are focusing on hiring highly creative employees so their organizations can survive in the global economy and the rapidly changing world. Educational institutions are seeing a need to teach creativity. Creativity is showing up in programs right from kindergarten up to graduate programs at universities. For example, several business departments at American universities such as the Graduate School of Business at Stanford University have a course in enhancing personal creativity.

"What's a cleb? It's a belc spelled backwards."

Creativity is the organization's competitive edge in today's rapidly changing world. It is the special talent that develops the right market segment. It is the ability that turns a crisis into an opportunity. It is the insight that recognizes a better and cheaper way to produce the company's existing product. It is innovation that helps a business prosper, while others fail.

The successful corporations in the immediate future will be the most innovative ones. Creativity precedes innovation. Innovation can only happen if organizations have highly creative employees. If you want to be a successful employee or entrepreneur, you will have to be one of these highly creative people.

Exercise - Creativity And You

1. Give a brief definition of creativity.

2. How can you profit from creativity in your career?

3. How can you profit from creativity in your personal life?

4. When was the last time you were creative? How?

.... Today

.... Yesterday

.... Last week

.... Last month or before

5. What inspires you to be creative?

6. In what type of environment are you most creative?

7. What principles do you consider important for becoming more creative?

Creativity Is Having Your Cake And Eating It Too

Just what is creativity? Posing this question to others always results in a number of interesting definitions. Here are some answers typical of those that I receive from the participants in my seminars:

- Creativity is being different.

- Creativity is the Mona Lisa.

- Creativity is thinking differently.

- Creativity is living happily unemployed.

- Creativity is being a genius.

- Creativity is having your cake and eating it too.

- Creativity is wanting to know.

- Creativity is being able to solve problems.

- Creativity is something children are good at.

- Creativity is playing a prank on a friend.

- Creativity is being unreasonable and crazy.

- Creativity is the ability to enjoy almost everything in life.

- Creativity is daydreaming at work without being caught.

- Creativity is being able to generate many options to just about any problem.

These are just a few of the many different definitions that are possible for creativity. All of the definitions represent some essence of the creative process. Even "creativity is being a genius" is appropriate since we all have some genius in us. The point is that creativity means different things to different people. Creativity is an experience and all our experiences are somewhat different. The myriad of definitions reflects the many sides of creativity.

6

My personal definition of creativity is "creativity is the joy of not knowing it all". The joy of not knowing it all refers to the realization that we seldom if ever have all the answers; we always have the ability to generate more solutions to just about any problem. Being creative is being able to see or imagine a great deal of opportunity to life's problems. Creativity is having many options. This book is about how to enhance our ability to generate opportunity and options that we would not otherwise generate.

In assigning a general definition to creativity, we can say that creativity is the ability to think or do something new. By new we do not mean new to all the world. We mean new to the person who is thinking or doing it. The ability to come up with something new is generally not a function of heredity, nor is it a function of an extremely high education.

Creativity can be learned. There is no magic associated with the ability to see more and come up with new ideas or solutions. Creativity is a skill that can be developed by just about everyone. It is a thinking skill, not difficult to master. But no matter what our level of mastery, it will remain a skill that we can always improve.

> *"Creativity is the sudden cessation of stupidity."*
>
> *- Dr. E. Land (Inventor of the Polaroid Camera)*

All being creative involves is first being aware of some basic principles and then using these principles in our lives. There are many benefits to be gained by both organizations and individuals from practicing creativity. The ultimate objective is to help you discover the genius within you. Then you can have your cake and eat it too. How? It's actually quite easy - just get yourself two cakes.

Seventeen (More Or Less) Principles Of Creativity

The following page lists the seventeen principles (more or less) that I consider basic for being creative at work or play. This means these principles can be applied to personal matters as well as career and business matters.

There is no claim here that these are the only available principles for enhancing your creativity. Other principles and techniques exist. The objective is to enhance your ability to see and generate more options by using as many techniques as possible.

Seventeen Principles Of Creativity

- Choose to be creative
- Look for many solutions
- Write your ideas down
- Fully analyze your ideas
- Define your goal
- See problems as opportunities
- Look for the obvious
- Take risks
- Dare to be different

- Be unreasonable
- Have fun and be foolish
- Be spontaneous
- Be in the now
- Practice divergent thinking
- Challenge rules and assumptions
- Delay your decision
- Be persistent

Don't Forget The Problem

Using the above principles of creativity to solve your problems will enhance both your career and personal life. In applying these principles of creativity to any problem, I must stress the importance of first identifying the problem. Let me give you an example of how I almost missed identifying the right problem. This could have cost me a lot of time and money and produced few, if any, results.

> *"The uncreative mind can spot wrong answers, but it takes a creative mind to spot wrong questions."*
>
> *- Anthony Jay*

When I was starting out in the seminar business, I sent out a brochure to company presidents and human resource managers. However, I wasn't getting much response from this brochure about my creativity seminars. So I decided my problem was my not having an interesting brochure. Before I spent money on an expensive brochure, I decided to kick around and study my problem. Eventually I realized my problem actually was how to get the attention and interest of the decision makers of organizations.

After realizing what my problem was, I asked this dumb question: Do I even need a brochure? No! Instead of spending more money on another brochure, which most people would have thrown away unread because of all the brochures they get, I created an exercise and sent it out in a letter. The following letter was used; it was twenty times as effective as mailing an expensive brochure.

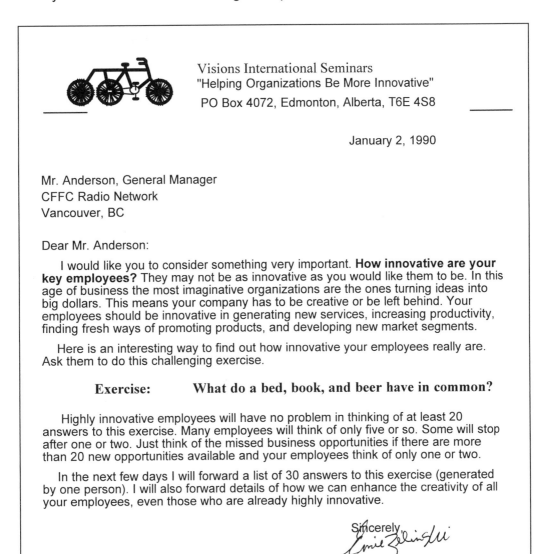

Visions International Seminars
"Helping Organizations Be More Innovative"
PO Box 4072, Edmonton, Alberta, T6E 4S8

January 2, 1990

Mr. Anderson, General Manager
CFFC Radio Network
Vancouver, BC

Dear Mr. Anderson:

I would like you to consider something very important. **How innovative are your key employees?** They may not be as innovative as you would like them to be. In this age of business the most imaginative organizations are the ones turning ideas into big dollars. This means your company has to be creative or be left behind. Your employees should be innovative in generating new services, increasing productivity, finding fresh ways of promoting products, and developing new market segments.

Here is an interesting way to find out how innovative your employees really are. Ask them to do this challenging exercise.

Exercise: **What do a bed, book, and beer have in common?**

Highly innovative employees will have no problem in thinking of at least 20 answers to this exercise. Many employees will think of only five or so. Some will stop after one or two. Just think of the missed business opportunities if there are more than 20 new opportunities available and your employees think of only one or two.

In the next few days I will forward a list of 30 answers to this exercise (generated by one person). I will also forward details of how we can enhance the creativity of all your employees, even those who are already highly innovative.

Sincerely,

Ernie J. Zelinski

Four Stages Of Creativity

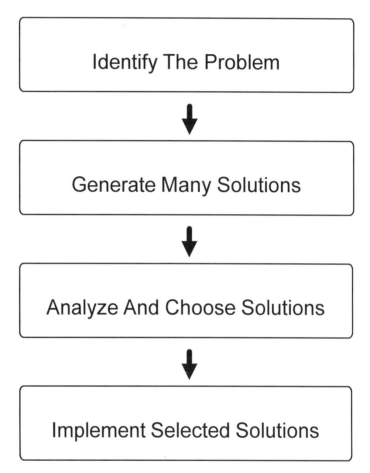

So don't forget to spend a little or even a lot of time just analyzing what your problem is. What's the use of generating a lot of brilliant solutions if you don't have a clue what the problem is?

After you have identified your problem, generated many solutions, and analyzed your solutions, you will be ready to implement your selected solutions. In the implementation stage you will invariably discover that another problem arises. Don't despair. This is an opportunity to be creative again by using the 17 principles of creativity in accordance with the four stages shown above.

1. How To Be Creative and Write Graffiti

Creativity All Around Us

Let us begin this chapter with the following two exercises.

Exercise #1-1 - Columbus And The Eggheads

At the Royal Court in Spain, Christopher Columbus asked the assistants if they could get an egg to stand on its end. They tried and could not do it. They thought it was impossible.

Columbus then said he could do it. The assistants bet him he could not. Columbus then proceeded to make the egg stand on its end. He collected his bet much to the frustration of the assistants.

What do you think Columbus did?

> "Some men see things as they are and ask, "Why?" I see them as they have never been and ask, "Why not?"
>
> - George Bernard Shaw

Exercise #1-2 - Creativity And Tardy Employees

The manager of a marketing department of a large corporation had a problem. Starting time was 8:00 o'clock. One of his employees was constantly late by about 30 minutes. She was the most creative and productive employee in the company.

The manager came up with a unique way of solving the problem.

How would you solve the problem of the tardy employee?

What You Know Is Not Creativity

Without any prior knowledge of the preceding exercises, did you generate some good new ideas for solving each one? (See chapter notes, page 20 for solutions.) Were there new thoughts in your solutions or were you searching for something that you already know? Keep this in mind: Creativity goes beyond what you already know. What you know is just knowledge.

Knowledge is not creativity; creativity transcends knowledge. This is an important distinction. Many people feel that grasping and remembering a myriad of facts and figures will give them the edge in life. This may give them the edge in trivial pursuits; however, having the edge in the important things in life is dependent on having the creative edge. The ability to think in new ways is much more important than the ability to remember what team won the Stanley Cup or which Fortune 500 company had the highest profits last year.

We have broadly defined creativity as the ability to come up with something new. How new were your ideas on how to stand an egg on its end or how to deal with a tardy employee? Knowledge of old ways is valuable; nevertheless, we must often look for fresh ideas if we are to find more effective solutions. Innovative thinking is approaching life's situations and problems in new ways so that these situations and problems are handled with greater ease.

"Imagination is more important than knowledge."

- Albert Einstein

New approaches are possible for just about anything. Abraham Maslow stated that a truly good soup can be as creative as a great painting or a marvelous symphony. Creativity can be found in music, painting, cooking, engineering, carpentry, accounting, law, economics, leisure, and sports. It has been with us through the ages and will continue to play an even more important role in our future development.

How Creative Are You Really?

Whether at work or play, you can be more creative. So the question is: How creative are you really? I would like you to do Exercise #1-3 which is the one I used in my letter shown on page 9.

Exercise #1-3

What do a bed, book, and beer have in common?

Note that highly creative individuals will have no problem in thinking of at least 20 answers to this exercise. Many people will think of only five or so. Some will stop after one or two. If you stopped after one or two solutions to this exercise, do you also stop after one or two solutions to your everyday problems at work or play?

If you thought of only one or two solutions to this exercise, you didn't put enough effort into solving it. After you look at my solutions (see chapter notes, page 20), you will see that the number of solutions to this exercise, as to many problems in life, is endless. You are missing out on many opportunities in your life if you are thinking of only one or two solutions when there are many solutions, or in some cases even an endless number.

"What a bed, book, and beer have in common is this crackpot Zelinski has used all of them in an exercise."

How you can use creativity at work and play is unlimited as well. Creativity can be found in every facet of human life. From the graffiti and the creative lawyer written about on the following pages to the examples cited in subsequent chapters, you will see many ways to use creativity for enhancing your life. Some of the benefits you will get from making the effort to be more creative include increased self-esteem, personal growth, more enthusiasm for solving problems, increased confidence to deal with new challenges, and different perspectives toward work and personal life.

Creativity Put In A Can

(The Creativity Of Good Graffiti)

Down with gravity

Bad spellers of the world, Untie!

Jesus saves!

(but Gretzky tips in the rebound)

I'd give my left arm to be ambidextrous

Reality is for those who cannot handle booze or drugs

Sex education is interesting but I never get any homework

Eve was framed

PLEASE DO NOT
FLUSH WHILE TRAIN
IS IN STATION

(Except in Pittsburgh)

Mickey Mouse is a rat

Roy Rogers was trigger happy

Power corrupts.
Absolute power is even more fun.

I'M SCHIZOPHRENIC
(So am I. That makes four of us)

I can't stand intolerance

My dad says they don't work

(written on contraceptive vending machine)

BILL STICKERS WILL BE PROSECUTED

(Bill Stickers is innocent. OK!)

Celibacy is not an inherited characteristic

Drink wet cement and get really stoned

We should hang all the extremists!

God is dead.
- Nietzsche
Nietzsche is dead.
- God

Humpty Dumpty was pushed

POINT OF VIEW IS RELATIVE
(Said Picasso to Einstein)

PREPARE TO MEET GOD!
(Jacket and tie, no jeans)

Isaac Newton was right!
This is the center of Graffiti

Death is natures way of telling you to slow down

DON'T LOOK UP HERE! THE JOKE IS IN YOUR HANDS!

(written above a urinal)

Graffiti's days are numbered. The writing is on the wall

WORST CHEWING GUM I HAVE EVER TASTED

(written on contraceptive vending machine)

{added} I agree, but, Oh! what bubbles!

BE ALERT!
Your country needs lerts

THE WORLD WILL END AT MIDNIGHT TONIGHT!
(12:30 in Newfoundland)

Peals of laughter
Screams of joy
I was here before Kilroy

Shut your mouth

Shut your face

Kilroy built the ruddy place

Even Lawyers Can Be Creative

The true account of the court action described below shows that lawyers, like everyone else, can be very creative.

On November 23, 1917 a Statement Of Claim was filed in the District Court Of Battleford by the plaintiffs, H. C. Humphrey and H. G. Chard, for damages to their female pig allegedly caused by a male pig owned by the defendant, Joseph Odishaw. The Statement of Claim, in part, read:

"I can't do no literary work for the rest of this year because I'm meditating another lawsuit and looking around for a defendant."

- Mark Twain

"That on or about the 4th day of November, 1917, a boar, the property of the defendant, was allowed by the Defendant to run at large contrary to the provisions of the said By-Law and the said boar broke and entered the lands of the Plaintiffs, being the lands above described, on or about the 4th day of November, 1917 and served a valuable sow of the Plaintiffs and the said sow became in pig to the great damage of the Plaintiffs.

The Plaintiffs therefore claim: $200.00 damages, and the cost of this action."

On January 14, 1918, the defendant's lawyer, A.M. Panton K.C., of the City of North Battleford filed a Statement of Defence. The third alternative in the Statement of Defence reads:

"In the alternative the Defendant says if his boar entered the close of the plaintiffs and had intercourse with the said sow that he did so at the solicitation of the said sow and that the said boar merely yielded to her blandishments and that she was solely guilty of the behavior complained of or is at least in "pari delicto" with the said boar and that her masters the said plaintiffs are guilty of an offence against the public morals in keeping a sow of such depraved habits to corrupt the morals of the neighborhood.

The Defendant waives his right to a counter-claim against the plaintiffs for lowering the vital powers of the said boar upon which the defendant might properly look for sustenance.

The Defendant therefore claims that this action be dismissed against him with costs."

Incidentally, there was no record of a trial or judgment in this case. Apparently the case was dropped or dismissed.

Is Your Brain Tilted Left or Right? - Does It Matter?

Creative thinking can be broken down into two types. Both types are important for the creative process.

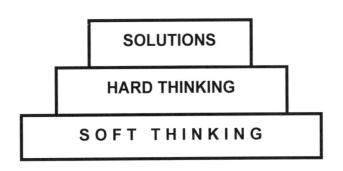

Soft Thinking - is the mode of thinking on which most of us can improve. Many artists and musicians are good at this type of thinking process. School systems and organizations normally frown at us if we think softly.

"So you're an artist. You guys have some sort of right-brain tilt, don't you?"

Soft thinking requires us to be flexible and random. It involves the unreasonable and the nonjudgmental. Humor and playfulness originate from soft thinking. This mode of thinking is valuable for generating a large number of ideas. Researchers say soft thinking is performed by the right side of our brains. Generally speaking, for problem solving soft thinking should be done before any hard thinking is started.

Hard Thinking - is the type of thinking most of us are pretty good at. It is analytical thinking for which school systems and organizations reward us.

This thinking mode makes us logical and practical. It is what our parents want us to be. Society also prefers us when we are logical and practical.

Hard thinking is needed for analysis of ideas. This is where we focus on usable solutions to our problems. We use hard thinking to put our plan into action. The left part of the brain is responsible for this thinking mode.

LEFT BRAIN	RIGHT BRAIN
practical	unreasonable
serious	playful
analytical	intuitive
structured	flexible
judgmental	nonjudgmental
orderly	random
HARD THINKING	**SOFT THINKING**

Solutions - require the two thinking processes for them to have both quality and quantity. The problem is that most of us don't use both styles of thinking effectively. Many of us use mainly the hard-thinking process, whereas some of us utilize mainly the soft-thinking process.

CREATIVE SUCCESS = HARD + SOFT THINKING

Innovative solutions are dependent on both modes of thinking. First we should generate many ideas using soft thinking. Then, using hard thinking processes, we should evaluate the ideas for their merits. Our end result should be several good options for the problem in question.

True creative thinking is a balance between soft and hard thinking, both used at appropriate times. Problem solving mainly through hard thinking isn't effective if there are few ideas with which to work. Similarly, it isn't effective to have generated a lot of ideas via soft thinking and not have properly analyzed and implemented these ideas.

It is important to note that the present trend to label people as either right-brain or left-brain thinkers is frowned upon by some researchers. The danger is that some people will have an excuse to limit themselves by using the right-brain or left-brain label to say something like: "Well I am a right-brained thinker and can't be any good at preparing and keeping to a budget."

The point is we all can enhance both our soft and hard thinking processes. Researchers have estimated every human brain has about 1 million, million or 1,000,000,000,000 braincells. When it comes to creativity, I know some people who appear to be using only about 1000 of these braincells and functioning at a modest IQ level of about 18.

> *"Don't mess with me, Rivers. I have an IQ of 160."*
>
> *- Famous ball player Jackson*
>
> *"Jackson, you can't even spell IQ."*
>
> *- Famous ball player Rivers*

Indeed, approximately 95 percent of people are dissatisfied with their mental performance. Researchers tell us most people use only 10 percent of their total brains, whether they are left-brain dominant or right-brain dominant. No wonder most of us aren't highly creative; we are wasting about 90 percent of our brains.

Whether we are right-brain dominant or left-brain dominant, we all have billions of underutilized braincells in both the dominant and the opposite hemispheres of our brains. We all can function better in those areas we claim we aren't good at. All it takes is a little effort.

Chapter Notes

Exercise #1-1

Columbus went into the kitchen and boiled the egg. Then he smashed the end of the egg on the table, causing the egg to stand on its end.

Of course, there are many other ways to stand an egg on its end. In my seminars we have come up with at least 20. For some of these solutions, see the Appendix, page 183.

Exercise #1-2

The manager gave the employee the only key to the office and made this employee in charge of seeing everyone else was on time.

We will see in Exercise #6-4 this problem has many solutions.

Exercise #1-3

Here are a few of the more obvious and boring solutions. You can hitchhike on these to generate some of your own.

> *"What's on your mind, if you will allow the overstatement?"*
>
> *- Fred Allen*

* All are represented by words which start with the letter "b".
* All have been advertised in magazines.
* All are sold.
* All go through a manufacturing process.
* All three are made for people to use.
* All are represented by words in the English language.
* All are represented by words which are nouns.
* All are represented by words having vowels and consonants.
* All are objects.
* All are represented by words which are one syllable and are singular.

For some more interesting solutions to this exercise see Appendix, page 183. From the 30 or so solutions I generated, you can see the number of solutions to this exercise is unlimited.

2. Robbed Blind By The Creativity Bandits

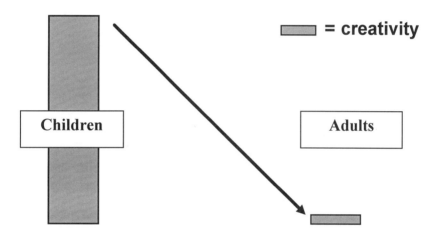

= creativity

Who Stole Your Creativity?

One evening my rambunctious nephew Cody, five years old at the time, was starting to get on my nerves. So I said to him: "Cody, that's enough; isn't it time you went to sleep? When do you go to sleep?" He looked at me and without hesitation said: "Not in a hundred million years." A little doubtful that he had convinced me, he quickly added "I don't go to bed until the morning." I was impressed. "Now that's creativity" I thought. Not many adults, if any, could come up with two creative answers like this in such a short time.

Adults often wonder why young children can have as much fun with the cardboard box a toy came in as with the toy itself. The answer: Children are just more creative than adults.

Most adults have become too structured in their thinking, especially towards having fun. They couldn't imagine there are so many interesting ways to enjoy a cardboard box.

Researchers confirm that children are much more creative than adults. What has happened to the creative abilities during those years in between childhood and adulthood? Obviously we encounter many barriers to expressing our creativity in the world around us.

> *"Adults are obsolete children."*
> - Dr. Seuss

In fact, it is worse than that. These walls act more like bandits than just barriers. By the time we are in mid-adulthood, nearly all of the creativity we had as children has been taken away by these culprits. *Business Week* some time ago reported that an adult of 40 is about 2% as creative as a child of 5.

Who are the responsible culprits who rob us blind of 98% of our creativity by the time we are 40 years old? Who can we blame?

The following exercise may give some clues.

Exercise #2-1 - To Logo Or Not To Logo

You are the new Manager of the Marketing Department of a fairly large company, Trane Computer Systems Ltd. Your boss, the General Manager of the company, has just come into your office and announced that the company wants to project a new image. She has asked you to personally design a new logo for the company. This new logo has to be done within two weeks.

You realize that the previous marketing manager was a commercial artist who did all the important art work. You believe that your background in art leaves a lot to be desired. All you know about art is what you took in elementary school. You have not done anything relating to art since. No one else in your department claims any more art ability than you do.

How would you respond to this task?

> *"I never let my schooling interfere with my education."*
> - Mark Twain

For the situation in the above exercise how did you react? Did you give some thought to designing the logo yourself? If you didn't, think why you chose to avoid the task. It could be due to those creativity bandits having robbed you of your willingness to undertake challenging and creative tasks. There are four great brain robbers:

The Four Great Brain Robbers

* 1. Society

* 2. Educational Institutions

* 3. Organizations

* 4. Ourselves

Societal Bandits Demand Your Conformity

> *"Conformity is the jailer of freedom and the enemy of growth."*
>
> *- John F. Kennedy*

If you decided to avoid designing the logo because you have no training in commercial art, you have allowed yourself to be a victim of societal programming. Cultural programming influences us to think that we have to possess a degree or formal training in a certain field to be able to accomplish anything worthwhile in that field. This thinking is absurd. Let us look at a few examples of the many people who accomplished things in fields in which they had no formal training.

* The *Coca-Cola* logo was designed by an accountant with no training in artwork.
* Eli Whitney, a school teacher, invented the cotton gin.
* Samuel Morse, an artist, invented the telegraph.
* Robert Campeau, a grade eight dropout, amassed a billion dollar department store empire (before he let his greed and ego lose most of it).
* The Wright Brothers invented the airplane. They were bike mechanics and not aeronautical engineers.
* The ballpoint pen was invented by a sculptor.

"Creating a disturbance! Not Guilty, Your Honor. I know I'm not creative."

Society's pressure to have us conform to its programming takes many forms and has many effects. Cultural taboos and tradition are followed to the detriment of new ideas. An over-emphasis on competition results in people doing things they would not otherwise do. Similarly, an over-emphasis on cooperation results in group think. Reason and logic are considered appropriate. Humor, intuition, and fantasy are not appreciated. All of these societal factors rob us of opportunities to be creative.

Educational Bandits Demand One Right Answer

You may have chosen not to design the logo in Exercise #2-1 because you wouldn't know the right way of going about it. Schools teaching us to look for the right way or the one "right" answer is an educational shortcoming. There are many right ways for designing logos as there are many answers to most problems. People leave school systems thinking there is a formula for everything when, in fact, the majority of problems can't be solved with formulas. More creative ways are needed. I have found going away from the formula to be most effective.

> *"In the first place God made idiots. That was for practice. Then he made school boards."*
>
> *- Mark Twain*

In most school systems reason and logic are over taught at the expense of other important matters. What the school systems ignore is that business decision making in today's world can't rely solely on reason and logic. Executive officers report using intuition in at least 40% of their major decisions. Yet consideration for the intuitive is absent from most school programs; so are the other creativity factors of vision, humor, and enthusiasm.

* Someone once asked the late inventor and philosopher, Buckminister Fuller, how he came to be a genius. He replied that he wasn't a genius. He stated that he had just not been as damaged by the school system as a lot of other people. He felt that the school system can damage us in many ways.

* Fred Smith who started the highly successful courier service, Federal Express, wrote a paper about the business before he started it. His professor did not think too highly of the idea and gave him a low mark in

> *"Education is very admirable but let us not forget that anything worth knowing cannot be taught."*
>
> *- Oscar Wilde*

the paper. Fortunately Fred Smith wasn't influenced by the over-intellectual assessment by the professor. His company is now one of the biggest and most innovative courier firms in the world.

Organizational Bandits Demean The Human Spirit

A lot of companies say they are innovative and supportive of creative people. Few really are. Saying the company is innovative sounds nice. These companies say they are innovative because this is the thing to say in this day and age. Looking at many companies' actions reveals a different story. The actions look more like an unconscious attempt to vandalize the creativity shown by the most innovative employees of the organization.

"Ms. Ford, with you being the manager, I was just thinking .... "

"Betty, I warned you about that."

Most of us wouldn't attempt to design the logo in the situation represented in Exercise #2-1 because of organizational factors which discourage creative attempts. Being creative involves risk taking. Risk taking is often something we avoid at work. The potential consequences scare us.

When a highly creative employee shows up at a company, the company often will not support his or her creativity. Highly innovative people question tradition, challenge the rules, suggest new ways of doing things, tell the truth about things and appear disruptive to the rest of the employees. The qualities that make these people innovative are usually frowned upon by the company. Attempts are made to transform the highly creative so they will behave like the less creative employees.

Group norms are protected at the expense of individual effort and ingenuity. Autocratic bosses discourage initiative. The organization sacrifices innovation and creativity to maintain a comfort level so it does not have to deal with the discomfort and disruptiveness necessary for innovation.

Although today's corporations need innovative employees to be highly successful, a lot of organizations end up robbing their employees of the opportunity to be innovative. Success eludes these organizations in the end.

Self Bandits - The Greatest Brain Robbers

We erect many individual barriers which also rob us of our creativity. Avoiding the design of a logo due to our lack of formal training in commercial art may be a result of fear. Fear of failure is one of the more effective robbers of our creativity. Along with fear stand laziness and perception. Both of these can interfere with our willingness to accept the challenge of designing a company logo or undertaking new projects in our lives.

> *"A man without imagination is like a bird without wings."*
>
> *- Wilhelm Raabe*

Laziness is due to a lack of self motivation. Motivational experts state that only 10% of the North American population is self or internally motivated. If we only allow ourselves to be externally motivated, we will not likely undertake the tasks needed to discover and recognize our creative abilities.

We generate many perceptions in our lives which are not necessarily representative of reality. The perception that we can't design a good logo because we have no formal training is a good example. This perception is false since most of us who aren't artistic are so because we haven't made the effort to be artistic. Once we make the effort, we all can design a logo.

Perception can distort many of life's realities. Let's look at the following exercises to see how easily our perception can interfere with the true picture.

> *"Honest criticism is hard to take, particularly from a relative, a friend, an acquaintance, or a stranger."*
>
> *- Franklin P. Jones*

Perception Can Be Deceiving

Exercise #2-2 - Looking At Perception

After you have taken quick glances at the four figures on the following pages, write down what you saw on a separate piece of paper.

Figure #2-1

Opportunity ISNOWHERE

Figure #2-2

Figure #2-3

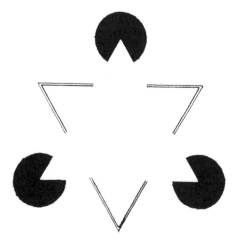

Figure #2-4

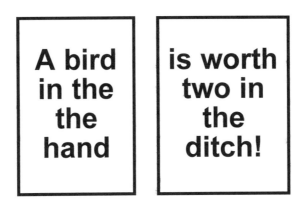

The above figures offer some proof that we don't always perceive things as well as we think we do.

If you looked at Figure #2-1 and saw only <u>Opportunity IS NOWHERE</u>, you haven't seen the opportunity in this figure. This can also stand for <u>Opportunity IS NOW HERE</u>.

Figure #2-2 is a photo of an advertisement for a woman's consumer trade show. This is an interesting example of what we can see if we take the time to look. Note there is a silhouette of a man's face in the woman's hair right under "Be all that you can be." Over 95% of the people will not see this with their first look. Was this silhouette by the artist intentional? What do you think?

In figure #2-3 you probably saw a triangle which is whiter than the rest of the page. Note that there is no actual triangle drawn there. Your eyes just imagined one being there based on the other figures. In addition, the whiteness of this mirage triangle is no brighter than the rest of the page.

If you saw everything there was to see in figure #2-4, you should have read the following in the two boxes.

A bird in the the hand is worth two in the ditch.

Not seeing the two the's is a case of not seeing what is actually there. In life we tend to do the same thing. We may see only one solution and not the many solutions that exist to our problems.

Classic Exercises With Non-Classic Solutions

Attempt the following exercises as a test of your creative abilities. You may have seen these exercises before. If you know a solution, then think up some others. Remember that creativity is going beyond what you already know to something new. Knowledge of the old is not creativity.

Exercise #2-3 - The "Old Nine Into Six" Trick

Change the Roman Numeral nine into a six by adding just one line.

(A solution appears in chapter notes, page 32.)

Exercise #2-4 - The "Classic Nine Circle" Exercise

Part A

Connect all the nine circles below using FOUR straight lines without lifting your pen or pencil from the surface. (If you can't solve this after 10 minutes, see chapter notes, page 32 for a hint.)

Part B

Now connect all the nine circles below using THREE straight lines without lifting your pen or pencil from the surface.

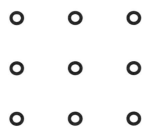

Part C

Now connect all the nine circles below using only ONE straight line without lifting your pen or pencil from the surface.

Chapter Notes

Exercise #2-3

The following solution is the standard one which is arrived at by overcoming the barriers to thinking that a line can only be a straight line and the six has to be in Roman numerals.

S I X

Many seminar presenters and motivational speakers use this exercise to emphasize creativity. However, they aren't very creative themselves, since they use the standard solution which they have seen somewhere. They aren't being creative; they are just sharing their knowledge acquired from someone else.

If seminar presenters using this exercise would have tried to be creative, they may have discovered there are at least seven more solutions to this exercise. See how many you can get. (Another solution appears in the Appendix, page 184.)

Exercise #2-4 - Part A

You won't solve this exercise if you haven't told the truth about the problem. Recall that the first stage of creativity is identifying the problem. If you placed an imaginary barrier around the nine circles, note that none exists. Until you start extending the straight lines outside the imaginary barrier, you may not solve the problem. (See Appendix, page 184 for a solution.)

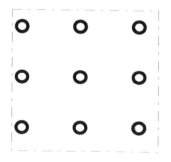

Exercise #2-4 - Parts B and C

See Appendix, page 184 for solutions.

3. Do Be Do Be Do

Lighting The Flame Rather Than Being Warmed By It

Exercise #3-1 - Having What It Takes To Be Creative

Which of the following factors is essential for us if we want to be creative?

_____ a) Being born creative

_____ b) Having had the right parents

_____ c) Having the right education

_____ d) Being right rather than left brained

_____ e) Having a high IQ

Creativity is thought to be a matter of special skill, ability, knowledge, or effort. In fact, it is none of these! Anyone can be creative. None of the above factors is an essential foundation for creative success. If you take a hard look at creative people, they are simply "being" creative. They are coming from excellence and creativity because they made the choice. There is no expectation of having some factor beyond their control make them creative. They realize they have to light the flame rather than be warmed by it.

"My life is filled with many obstacles. The greatest obstacle is me."

- Jack Parr

HAVE ➡ DO ➡ BE

"I was fired from my last job for being too creative. I tried to design an off switch for a perpetual motion machine."

There are those who believe that the above sequence represents the road to creativity. Their belief is that a person must first "HAVE" what creative people have: inherited intelligence, high education, a good job, money and a host of other things. Then the person will "DO" what creative people do. Finally the person will "BE" creative. This belief is false. There is no truth to the belief that creative people have special things that enable them to be creative and non-creative people do not have these things. The fact of the matter is non-creative people have all the things necessary to be creative.

Reversing the above sequence better represents the road to creativity. The right order is from "BEING" to "DOING" to "HAVING".

BE ➡ DO ➡ HAVE

"To be is to do."
    - Camus

"To do is to be."
    - Sartre

"Do be do be do."
    - Frank Sinatra

First, we must choose to "BE" creative. Then, we will "DO" the things creative people do. What will follow naturally is we will "HAVE" the things that creative people have. The "HAVE" things include the ability to cope with and enjoy a rapidly changing world. There is also the sense of accomplishment, satisfaction, and happiness generated from attempting and completing challenging activities.

The major difference between creative people and non-creative people is two fold. First, creative people believe that they can be creative. They know that creativity can be learned. Creative people do not deny their abilities and potentials. Second, creative people know they have to get themselves moving. They realize that they have to choose to be creative.

People Choosing To Be Creative

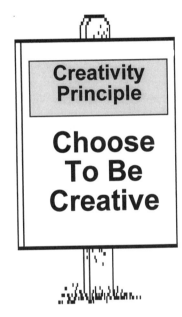

*   A few years ago Ted Endicott was the top retail car salesperson for General Motors anywhere. In one 11-month period he had sold 456 cars. His sales averaged about 40 cars a month. Not too bad considering that the national average is about 10 cars a month. Endicott's 1987 earnings were $125,000. The one thing you should know about Endicott is that he became blind after selling cars for 27 years. Did he quit? No he didn't. He chose to adjust to his handicap. His impressive sales continued due to his creativity in dealing with his handicap. Most customers didn't realize he was blind until after the sale.

*   Pam Chorley owns Fashion Crimes, one of Toronto's most bizarre businesses. The Canadian designer specializes in creating "fashion don'ts". Her Fashion Crimes store has featured alternative fashions which ignore the trendy fashions most women are programmed to adopt. Chorley defies the rules and designs ladies' fashions so weird that several people entering her store for the first time have asked her if she had actually ever sold anything since she opened. In fact, Chorley has sold a few things. She has been operating the store for over ten years and has just opened her second store called Misdemeanours, which also specializes in alternative fashions, but only for infants.

Are You Too Intellectual To Be Creative?

"There are some things only intellectuals are crazy enough to believe."

- George Orwell

Seymour Epstein, a psychologist at the University of Massachusetts, has found that constructive thinking is crucial for life success. Constructive thinking has almost nothing to do with our IQ. Constructive thinking involves taking action about a situation rather than complaining about it. It also involves the ability not to take things personally and not to fret about what others think of us. Constructive thinking determines a great range of life's successes, from salaries and promotions, to happiness with friendships, to physical and emotional health.

Epstein found that many academically bright people do not think constructively. They have self-destructive habits of mind. They hold back from new challenges because they lack the necessary emotional smarts. Emotional intelligence was found by Epstein to be more important than academic intelligence.

Epstein's findings shouldn't surprise many of us. We are already aware that many people with PhD's are not very creative and some of the most creative people around don't even know what a PhD is.

"There is nothing so irritating as somebody with less intelligence and more sense than we have."

- Don Herold

Why don't more people choose to be constructive thinkers? My personal theory is that it is because becoming a constructive thinker takes effort and change. Most people resist anything that requires effort or change. Given the choice of doing something that is easy or something that is difficult, most people will opt for the easy. Why? Short term comfort appeals to most people.

The choice of comfort is a paradox. Choosing to avoid the difficult is more comfortable in the short term; however, in the long term it results in discomfort. Most of us need to have tackled and conquered challenging tasks before we experience a sense of accomplishment and satisfaction.

So Much For The Easy Life

One of the biggest reasons for people being uncreative is their reluctance to take risks. People take the no-risk route because it is the most comfortable. All of us have the tendency to seek comfort at some time or other. In fact, most of us take the comfortable way all the time. The problem with choosing the comfortable way is in the long run it turns out to be very uncomfortable. This is best explained by what I call the "EZ (Easy) Rule Of Life."

Figure #3-1 represents this rule. What it says is when we choose the easy and comfortable route, life turns out to be difficult. Ninety percent of people choose this route because short-term comfort is the most appealing.

The other option is to take the difficult and uncomfortable route. When we choose the difficult and uncomfortable route, life is easy. Ten percent of people take this route because they know they must experience short-term discomfort for long-term gains. They also know there is much less competition than on the other route. Guess which route I had to travel to create a bestselling book?

Figure #3-1 - The EZ Rule Of Life

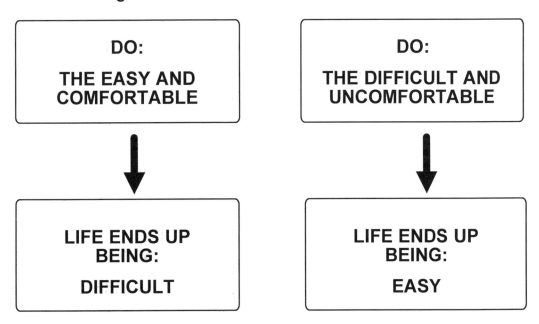

In The Real World It's Publish and PROMOTE or Perish

Many people have written or phoned me due to the success of my self-published book, *"The Joy Of Not Working"*. Most of these people think I have found the easy way to make a book a best-seller; however, The EZ Rule Of Life applies here.

Visions International Publishing
"Learning Resources For Business & Leisure"
P.O. Box 4072, Edmonton, Alberta, T6E 4S8

Dear Aspiring Author:

So you want to be a successful writer with a best-seller or two. Contrary to what most people believe, I don't have a secret formula for making a book a best-seller. However, I can offer some basic advice which I consider extremely important for creating a best-seller.

First and foremost if you want to write a bestselling book because you think it is an easy way to fame and fortune, do yourself a favor by pursuing something else immediately. Writing a book and making it a best-seller is much more difficult than getting an undergraduate university degree, going on to a masters degree, topping it up with a doctorate degree, and finally landing a job as hard as it is to land a job today. Don't believe me? Just remember that there are a lot more people with doctorate degrees than there are people who have written bestselling books. Besides, if it was so easy to create a bestselling book, practically everyone would be doing it. If you haven't noticed, about 99% of the people always take the easy way out in life. That's why they will never have a bestselling book.

Here is the second important test: How good are you at celebrating failure and being motivated by criticism and rejection? Creating a best-seller will require that you accept and celebrate failure. Writing and promoting a book to make it a best-seller will require that you are not only able to cope with, but more importantly, be motivated by criticism and rejection. For example, when *The Joy Of Not Working* made the Globe and Mail's list of books that definitely would <u>not</u> be reviewed by their book section, I was motivated to show them that my book would outsell 99% of all the books they review.

The letter I send to all people who contact me about publishing is presented on these two pages. The main point is that it takes creativity and effort to establish a best-seller. Creativity and effort are required not only in writing a book; but also for promoting the book. This requires doing the difficult and uncomfortable instead of the easy and comfortable.

If you have passed the above two tests with flying colors, then there may be hope for you. Now go out and buy and read all the books you can find on writing, publishing, and promotion (Note, I said BUY these books, not borrow them - if you won't buy someone else's books, why should you expect anyone to buy yours?)

Next, what are you going to write about? The most important principle here is to select a topic for which there is a market. You have to first ask yourself: "Who is going to want to buy my book?" Then you better have a damn good answer.

Just because you think people should be reading books in your chosen topic doesn't mean there will be a market for your book. Don't fall into the trap like so many people (including major publishers) who go on the basis of what they think other people should be reading. Your opinion of what is important, or what ought to be important to people, is totally irrelevant. The people who buy books are the ones who will decide what is important to them. This is the way it should be; it's their money.

Once you have completed a book and had it published, you are about 5% of the way there to making it a best-seller. Whether the book is self-published or published by a major publisher, you must promote your product. You can have the best product in the world, but if you can't market it, you may as well have the worst product. The best promotion for a book is not done by publishers, distributors, or bookstores; the best promotion is done by the author. In the academic world, it's publish or perish. In the real world, it's publish and PROMOTE or perish.

Writing a good book takes creativity; effective promotion takes ten times as much creativity. Two years after I wrote *The Joy Of Not Working* I am still promoting the book with the same level of effort and creativity as when the book was first released. I will be doing this for at least another 3 years.

Another very important point: You have to start by doing. All the knowledge in the world isn't going to help you if you don't do something with it.

Finally, I could wish you luck but I won't - luck isn't what will get you there. Your own motivation, determination, and creativity will get you there.

Sincerely,

Ernie Zelinski

Ernie J. Zelinski

Don't Pay The Price; Enjoy The Price

> *"If people knew how hard I worked to get my mastery, it wouldn't seem so wonderful at all."*
>
> *- Michelangelo*

Let me warn you that The EZ Rule of Life is something like the law of gravity. Mess around with the law of gravity by walking off the top of a building and see what happens to you. It knocks you on your butt. The same thing applies with the EZ Rule Of Life. Mess around with it by taking the easy way and you wind up on your butt as well. It seems to work all the time. Note, this is the way life is. Please don't blame me for the way it is; I didn't set it up this way. I just observed that life is this way and we have to make the best of it.

The biggest obstacle to success is the discomfort in doing the necessary things we must do to attain success. As human beings we gravitate towards less pain and more pleasure. The majority of us opt for the easy way because we are seeking comfort at all costs. Roads on which there is a lot of traffic tend to have a lot of ruts.

Choosing the easy way in life ensures we wind up in one or more of these ruts. And the only difference between a rut and a grave are the dimensions. In the rut you get to join the "living-dead", and in the grave you get to join the "dead-dead".

Everything in life has a price. Most people take the course of inaction because at the time it seems the easiest. In the end they cheat themselves out of the big payoffs. Take my advice and don't be one of the majority who choose comfort at the expense of accomplishment and satisfaction. The real prizes in life come to us when we are willing to do things somewhat difficult and uncomfortable. Choosing to be creative is one of them.

There is a price to pay in making the effort to be creative, just as there is in anything worthwhile in life. But rather than looking at the price we have to pay, let us look at the many "prices we get to enjoy". Prices to enjoy include: higher self-esteem, greater satisfaction, increased happiness, and more peace of mind. Indeed the price is to be more enjoyed than paid. Creativity involves doing the difficult and uncomfortable; the payoff is that it is much more rewarding and satisfying than doing the easy and comfortable.

4. 101 Ways To Skin A Cat Or Do Just About Anything

Getting The "Right Answer" May Put You On The Wrong Track

Let us begin this chapter with the following two exercises.

Exercise #4-1

Big Rock Brewery Ltd. of Calgary couldn't afford the traditional beer marketing promotions large breweries use when it was about to introduce its beer products to the extremely competitive markets in Canada and United States. Big Rock has been able to introduce its products with great success and have sales grow substantially while Canada's big breweries have been consolidating and battling over a shrinking market.

How would you have handled the problem of little money for advertising to launch new beer products in a competitive and shrinking market?

> *"There ain't no answer. There ain't going to be any answer. There never has been an answer. That's the answer."*
>
> *- Gertrude Stein*

Exercise #4-2 - The Unique Pair Of Scissors

Which pair of scissors is different from all the others?

A

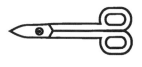

B

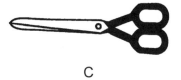

C

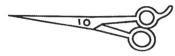

D

E

A North American and a European were discussing the joys of life when the European stated that he knew 100 different ways to make love. The North American was highly impressed with this. He told the European he knew only one. The European asked him which one it was. The North American described the most natural and conventional way there is. The European then replied to the North American "That is amazing! I never thought of that! Thanks. Now I know 101."

> *"I once made love for an hour and fifteen minutes but it was the night the clocks are set ahead."*
>
> *- Garry Shandling*

Are you like the North American or the European when solving problems? Do you come up with only one solution or many? We have all heard the saying "there is more than one way to skin a cat." Yet how many of us would look for several ways to skin a cat if we had to skin one.

Most of us are apt to look for one way to do most tasks. If this single way does not work well, we still stick with it and find someone or something to blame for the situation being unworkable. We do not look for new ways. Another way may be quicker, more efficient, or less costly. Last, but not least, it could plainly be more fun. Ask the European if you ever run into him.

> *"After watching these game shows for over 10 years, I have yet to answer one question correctly."*

Let us return to Exercise #4-1. Were you looking for the one right way of overcoming the problem? Did you stop after one solution or did you come up with many alternatives?

How Big Rock Brewery Ltd. handled it is not the only way (see chapter notes, page 48). Many solutions are available. The management of Big Rock could have borrowed money for advertising. They could have sold shares in the company to generate additional money for advertising. Partnership with an established brewery was an option, as was generating publicity through some off-beat activity. The list of options is endless.

> *"There are nine ways of poaching eggs, and each of them is worse than the other."*
>
> *- Robert Lynd*

Exercise #4-2 gives more evidence of how we approach problems. Did you overlook the obvious like nine out of ten people do on this exercise? Ninety percent of participants in my seminars end up choosing one of the five pairs of scissors. Everyone is right to a certain degree, but most participants miss the main point. That is because the answer is *"all the pairs of scissors are different from all the others"*.

This exercise demonstrates how well the school systems have taught us to automatically look for the one right answer or one way of doing things. In doing so, we become very structured in our responses. We tend to stop looking for more "right answers". When the only "right" answer we come up with is a "dud", we are lost.

One of the most important creativity principles is there are two or more solutions to all problems. Two exceptions to the rule exist. One is in mathematics. Half of 13 has only one answer. (Note we will see in Chapter 9 that even this problem may have more than one solution.) In mathematics most problems have one solution. The only other time there are less than two solutions is when we are dead. Then there are no solutions. Generally speaking, life's problems have two or more solutions.

Possibility in life's situations extends beyond the available and obvious. What do we have to do to create many new solutions? It is essential we first let go of the old and go to a state of nothing. Yes, we must start from nothing. Opportunity is literally created from a state of nothingness. When we let go of old solutions and old ways of thinking, we have a clear slate from which we can create.

Break It Before Someone Else Breaks It

Looking for options requires effort. It is easier to look for alternatives when we are dissatisfied with the alternatives we have at hand. However, we should look for more solutions even when the ones we already have appeal to us. Care should be taken in not necessarily limiting ourselves to the first few alternatives we generate. Disciplining ourselves to keep looking for other alternatives, even when we are satisfied with some of those already generated, is a good practice.

Creativity Principle

Look For Many Solutions

The point is that better solutions and alternatives should be strived for even when things appear to be going well. Attempts at inventing better alternatives when a good one is already available has three main benefits:

* This provides some insurance that a better alternative has not been overlooked. The successful alternative in use may not be the best available.

* Most, if not all, good things come to an end. People, who generate alternatives when things are going well, have other solutions to fall back on when the present solution is no longer effective due to changing circumstances.

* People continually involved in the selection of alternatives, whether needed or not, will keep their creative talents in practice for when they are needed.

The old adage "If it works, don't fix it" is questionable in this day and age. Even if it is working fine, it probably won't for very long in a competitive and rapidly changing business world. Having the ability to generate many solutions allows us to react much more effectively when it does break down.

"Doing the same thing over and over, expecting different results is the definition of crazy."

- Unknown Wise Person

Robert J. Kriegel and Louis Patler in their book *"If it ain't broke .... Break It!"* go so far as to say break it before it breaks on its own, or before someone else breaks it. Following Kriegel's and Patler's philosophy will help you be innovative and put you way ahead of 99% of the people who will wait for it to break down before they attempt to fix it.

Exercises To Motivate You To Look And Look And Look

Exercise #4-3   - Triangles Galore (If you look)

The diagram below is a perspective builder. You simply have to count the number of triangles in the diagram. (See chapter notes, page 48 when you are finished.)

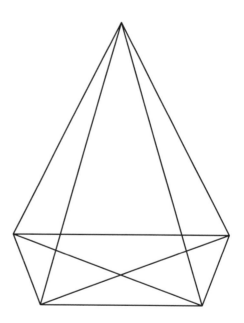

Exercise #4-4 - Playing With Matches

In preparation for the next chapter, let us try another type of exercise. Assume the following two equations are made with match sticks. Each line in the characters is one match stick. Both equations are wrong as they stand. Can you by moving just one match stick in each equation make the equations correct? Start with (a) and only proceed to (b) when you have completed (a). (See chapter notes, page 48 when you are finished both.)

(a)

$$VI + II = VI$$

(b)

$$VI - IV = IX$$

Exercise #4-5 - A Quota Of New Ideas

Do this exercise regularly. Set a goal to generate at least 3 new ideas daily for your most important project or problem.

Chapter Notes

Exercise #4-1

Big Rock Brewery Ltd. first focused on the huge Californian market by introducing products with unorthodox beer names such as Buzzard Breath, Warthog Ale, and Albino Rhino. At the time of my writing this book, Big Rock has introduced a new product called Grasshopper Ale. A large part of Big Rock's success has been their names. As Big Rock's USA distributor, Bill Gibbs of Claymore Beverage says: "Warthog Ale just lunges off the shelf at you."

> *"In the republic of mediocrity, genius is dangerous."*
>
> *- Robert Ingersoll*

Big Rock has established credibility at the high end of the market in the trendy professional restaurants by targeting promotions at theatre groups, folk festivals, ballet, and opera instead of the traditional groups which the large breweries go after. Big Rock's beers sell at a premium of $15.00 a case in comparison to the $10.00 to $12.00 a case the large breweries charge for their products.

Exercise #4-2

They are all different from all the others.

Exercise #4-3

Most people see fewer than 25 triangles in this figure. There are 35 triangles if you really look.

Exercise #4-4

Did you proceed to (b) after getting only one solution for (a)? These two exercises are a test for how well you mastered the principle of looking for more than one solution. Notice how easy it is to stop after only one solution. If you didn't get at least 3 solutions to both exercises, you are in the majority.

Exercise (a) has at least 30 solutions and (b) has at least five. Now go back and try again. If you attend one of my creativity seminars, I will show you several blockbuster solutions to exercise (a) which only one in 1000 people will see.

5. A Great Memory For Forgetting

Is Your Photographic Memory Out Of Film?

How good is your memory? The intent of this chapter is to underscore the importance of writing our ideas down. We have a tendency to avoid writing down ideas thinking that we will remember them later. This is a mistake. We aren't as good at remembering things as we think we are.

The following exercises will demonstrate this.

Exercise #5-1 - I'm Too Old To Remember That!

Draw the dial of a non-digital telephone, that is one having a rotary dial rather than a touch-tone one. Place all the finger holes in their right position on the dial and then record the position of all the numbers and letters. This is something that you have seen many times so it won't be a problem to remember, right!

If you think you are too young (or too old) to remember the rotary telephone, try this exercise with a modern digital telephone. Try to remember the numbers and the corresponding letters which go on the different keys.

> "I always have trouble remembering three things: faces, names, and ... I don't remember what the third thing is."
>
> - Fred Allen

Now refer to the back of this chapter (page 56) to see how well you did on the above exercise. If you didn't get the layout of the non-digital telephone (or the digital one) completely, you are definitely in the majority. Most of us have a hard time remembering what either dial precisely looks like. Let us try another exercise.

Exercise #5-2 - Remembering A Robbery

Recall the cartoon with the two robbers in Chapter #2. Assume you witnessed that attempted robbery and have been asked by the police department to identify the two robbers. Without looking back at the cartoon on page 22, try to pick the two men out of the 12 in the following figure who were attempting the creativity robbery.

By now some of you are probably getting worried about your memories being shot because of your age. Not so. Look at children. Ask a school teacher whether children forget things at school. The school teacher will list things like coats, lunch pails, gloves, books, combs, pencils, pens, and much more. Children don't forget because of their age; neither do we. We forget because of the many distractions we have in our lives.

> *"I never forget a face, but in your case I'll be glad to make an exception."*
>
> *- Groucho Marx*

"Almost anything you do today will be forgotten in just a few weeks," states John McCrone in the March, 1994 issue of *New Scientist*. "The ability to retrieve a memory decays exponentially, and after only a month more than 85 percent of our experiences will have slipped beyond reach, unless boosted by artificial aids such as diaries and photographs."

Not remembering the dial on the telephone or the two faces in a picture is not a serious thing. However, forgetting good ideas for our problems may cost us wonderful or blockbuster solutions. Ideas are easy forgotten. Exercise #5-3 may give more evidence of this.

Exercise #5-3 - Thinking About Your Past Thinking

Write down the thoughts that you were thinking at exactly this time of the day one week ago. In addition, write down all the good ideas you had about solutions to your problems, someone else's problems, or to society's problems in the last week.

How did you do? If you could not remember much about what you were thinking one week ago, how do you know if you have forgotten one or more blockbuster ideas that you had right at that time? How about all the ideas during the week since then? Possibly you had some useful ideas that you didn't write down and have since forgotten.

To deal with the tendency of their employees forgetting good ideas, some organizations have installed locker rooms in their work premises. Writing pads and pens have been placed in these locker rooms. These are for recording ideas that the employees may think of while exercising or in the shower. There is a good reason for this practice. Many good ideas are generated when people exercise. Good ideas tend to come from the altered states of mind that exercise produces. The companies want to be sure that the ideas are recorded immediately and not lost with time.

If our ideas are not recorded immediately, we risk not recalling them later. What causes this tendency to not recall ideas at a later time is our changed state of mind. Our minds are overworked trying to remember the many things for everyday living. When we become totally engrossed in something else related to other work assignments or to our personal lives, the last thing on our minds are the good ideas we had one or two days ago while in the shower.

To totally convince yourself about the importance of recording your ideas and solutions, do one last exercise over a period of time. When you are working on a special project, write down all the ideas that you get and put them in a file. Be extremely disciplined about this. Don't forget to record anything. Do this for two weeks and during these two weeks do not review the contents of the file. At the end of the two weeks try and remember everything that went in the file. Then look in the file. You may be surprised at the number of ideas that you have forgotten.

Growing An Idea Tree

Writing your ideas, answers, and solutions for a special problem or project can be done in many different forms. You can either make a list, use sentences, or write an essay. These all have their places; however, there is a better tool for recording ideas. This device is especially useful in the initial stages of solving the problem or working on a project.

> *"I finally got it all together and then I forgot where I put it."*
>
> *- Anon*

The tool is an idea tree. Other names by which this tool is also known include mind map, spoke diagram, thought web, and clustering diagram. The idea tree is simple but powerful. The surprising thing is that most of us were never shown how to use an idea tree when attending our educational institutions. I first learned about it from a waiter in a restaurant.

Here is how an idea tree is created. Starting at the center of the page, the goal, theme, or purpose of the idea tree is recorded. For example, if you are generating an idea tree for the ways in which you want to market a new management book, you can write this down as in Figure 5-1.

From the central theme, branches or lines are drawn towards the boundary of the page. On these branches are printed any ideas that relate to the problem or project. Primary ideas are recorded on separate branches near the center of the page. Secondary branches are then drawn exiting from the primary ones. This is where the secondary ideas that relate to the main ones are recorded. More branches off the secondary ones can be drawn which will record a third level of ideas.

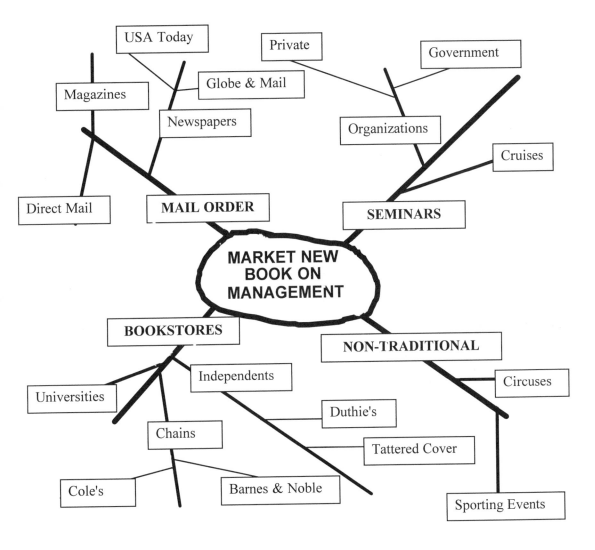

Figure 5-1

An Idea Tree For Generating Ideas On How To Market A New Book On Management

> *"A man would do well to carry a pencil in his pocket, and write down the thoughts of the moment. Those that come unsought for are commonly the most valuable, and should be secured, because they seldom return."*
>
> *- Francis Bacon*

One primary idea for marketing a new management book is to market the book in bookstores. The word "Bookstores" is recorded as one of the primary ideas on the idea tree in Figure 5-1. Then secondary ideas are generated to enlarge on the types of bookstores. Chains, university, and independent bookstores are listed on the second level of ideas. A third level of ideas is used to enlarge on the chain bookstores. Here we include the Barnes & Noble's and the Cole's bookstore chains. More levels of ideas can be added if needed.

This tool is a powerful way of generating a lot of ideas quickly. Although the idea tree is meant to be a tool for individual brainstorming, it can be adapted for group use without any problems. Let us look at the reasons for the effectiveness of the idea tree as an idea-generating tool.

Advantages Of The Idea Tree

* It is compact. Many ideas can be listed on one page. If needed, the idea tree can be expanded to additional pages.

* Ideas are put in categories. This makes it easier to group ideas.

* The creator of an idea tree can hitchhike on his or her own ideas to generate many other ideas. This works in much the same way as hitchhiking in group brainstorming.

* It is a long-term tool. After setting it aside for a day or a week, the person using the tree can come back and generate a batch of fresh ideas.

Idea trees are not only used for the right-brain activity of rapid idea generation. Another way to use an idea tree is for the purpose of self-discovery by way of clustering thoughts about such things as what your relationship is with money.

Left-brain activities such as planning and organizing also lend themselves to being performed on idea trees. Short-range plans, long-range plans, diaries, speech plans, goals, and records of lecture notes can be done with this useful tool.

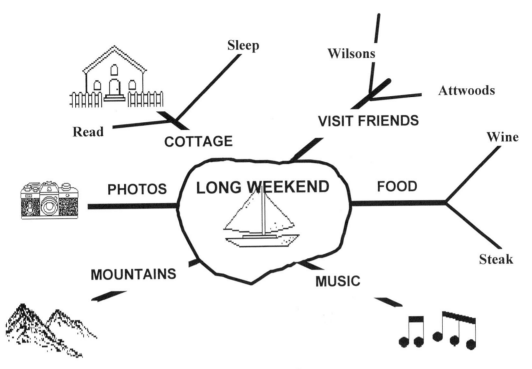

Figure 5-2

An Idea Tree (Using Visuals) For Generating Ideas On What To Do On A Long Weekend

Figure 5-2 shows a more advanced idea tree which uses images. Images are used to enhance creativity and memory. Color can be used along with images to add to the effects of the idea tree.

Idea trees require more work than do ordinary lists; however, the extra work is well worth it. Remember "The EZ Rule Of Life" from Chapter 3. By putting in the extra work in constructing this more difficult and challenging tool, you will be a lot better off in the long run than you are with ordinary lists or by not using any tool at all.

Who of major consequence has used idea trees? Only such people as Albert Einstein, Leonardo Da Vinci, Thomas Jefferson, John F. Kennedy, and Thomas Edison. I think this is a good group with which to be associated.

Chapter Notes

Exercise #5-1

Not one in a thousand people in my seminars will get this
exactly. Note that there are some things you did not notice about
the rotary telephone dial even though you have seen it many
times. These are things that were staring you in the face but you
never saw. Why? You never put in the effort to look. Similarly
many solutions to our problems stare us in our faces. We do not
see these solutions because of our lack of effort in looking.

    a) The 1 has no letters beside it.

    b) The Q and Z are not used.

    c) The letters go clockwise in ABC, DEF, GHI, and
       JKL. The letters go counterclockwise in all the other
       sets of three letters.

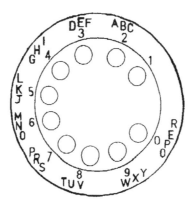

As you can see, the layout of the digital telephone is not much
easier to remember.

56

6. The Advantages Of Drinking On The Job

Cycle Designed By A Psycho?

The best way to emphasize the point of this chapter is to start with the following exercise.

Exercise #6-1

You have been hired by a major bicycle manufacturer as a consultant. Your job is to evaluate the merits of the bicycle designs that designers submit to the manufacturer. The manufacturer has asked for a new design for a tandem bicycle.

One of the designs that the manufacturer received is my design shown above. Although my undergraduate degree is in electrical engineering, I decided I could design something mechanical. (I know you are impressed.)

Write down the main points about my design for a new tandem bicycle that you will put in your report to the manufacturer. Be honest in your evaluation and don't be afraid of hurting my ego.

Let's look at my bicycle design in Exercise #6-1. What points did you choose for your report? Are your points all negative? If they are, you haven't fully explored my design. Unless you put down some positive points, some negative points, and some in between, you have jumped to conclusions without due consideration to my "wonderful" design. Your voice of judgment (VOJ) has stepped in too soon.

"Good judgment comes from experience; and experience, well, that comes from bad judgment."

- Unknown Wise Person

You should have considered such positive points as the rear wheel can be used as a spare for the front in case the front tire goes flat. How about a more comfortable ride because of two back wheels? This bicycle could also have an advantage over conventional ones for carrying heavy loads. It is great for overweight people. People may want to buy it as a status symbol since it is a new and different design.

On the negative side, the bicycle may be awkward to ride. The back wheel may be excess baggage. It looks ridiculous. There is no second seat for an extra person.

There are many points to be made for both the positive and negative aspects of this design. To fully explore the merits of this design, we should write down and consider all these points. Then we can make a decision based on a comprehensive evaluation of this new idea for a bicycle.

Exercise #6-2

You are the owner of a medium size advertising agency. To remain competitive, your company is looking for new markets and new opportunities. Two weeks ago you introduced a suggestion box to encourage new ideas from the employees. As you are going through the latest ideas in the suggestion box, a rather odd suggestion appears. The suggestion says "Our new promotional flyers belong in washroom stalls."

What should you do with this suggestion?

1. Assume it is a practical joke, chuckle and disregard it.

2. Assume the idea is serious but the originator is demented.

3. Assume it means that the new flyers are ineffective.

4. Assume the idea is serious and has some merits.

Don't Nuke Your Ideas With VOJ

Your voice of judgment (VOJ) may have affected the answer that you chose in Exercise #6-2? Did you choose to ignore or eliminate the washroom stalls as a viable advertising medium? If you did, think again. An entrepreneur in the USA is generating millions of dollars of revenue annually by selling advertising space in washrooms of businesses and airplanes. The idea was spawned when he left sales brochures in washrooms and he started getting great responses. One of the biggest advantages is that the audience is more captive with this form of advertising. If you did not give this advertising medium any consideration, it is because you were the victim of your voice of judgment. This prevented you from fully exploring this idea.

> **Creativity Principle**
>
> # Fully Analyze Your Ideas

We are all victims of our voices of judgment. This is the rational part of us that can jump in and destroy an idea before it has a chance to blossom. Many good ideas are not given full consideration. We tend to find something negative about these ideas and promptly discard them. The reverse is also true. We may promptly accept an idea without looking at all the negatives.

Some Great "Wacky" Ideas Saved From VOJ

Many successful ideas have been spared death by others' VOJ because the originators of these ideas had the presence of mind to fully explore them for their value. Most people in our society would not have given these ideas any consideration at all. Yet due to the ideas' success, they are taken for granted as being the norm today.

* By accidently preparing grain too long, the Kellogg brothers in the late 1800s wound up with a new product which they decided to introduce as a cold cereal. Until then cereal was always eaten hot. Most marketing experts predicted imminent failure for this product which they labelled "Horsefood". The Kelloggs called this product, still popular today, "cornflakes".

* Over ten years ago, Bill Comrie along with two partners took over his father's small furniture sales store in Edmonton, Alberta. Today Bill Comrie owns the Brick Furniture stores which comprise one of the biggest furniture chains in North America. One of Comrie's first marketing tools was the "Midnight Madness Sale." The first one he proposed was questioned by his two partners. They claimed no one would show up. Well, show up they did. The furniture store did more business during that one night than Bill Comrie's father had done in the previous year in the store. The "Midnight Madness Sale" was used with great success in the early days of The Brick's phenomenal growth.

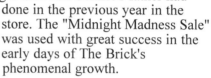

"Darn it, why didn't I think of this ingenious bicycle?"

* On the night that the idea for the Pet Rock was conceived, several people laughed and joked about this great pet that everyone would want. Of course, this was a ridiculous idea to everyone except for Gary Dahl. He went home and could not sleep because of the idea's promise. It was then that he overcame his VOJ and decided to market a book giving instructions on how to care for a Pet Rock. Its success is history.

* Even Post-It Notes almost got nuked by VOJ. The idea of Post-It Notes originated in 1974 with Art Fry, a 3M employee who sang in a choir. He used bits of paper to mark the hymns but the papers kept falling out of his books. He went into the office one day and made some papers with adhesive backing. These worked well. When 3M decided to look into marketing a commercial variation of these notes, distributors thought they were silly. Initial market surveys offered little promise. The 3M company did not allow others' voices of judgment to interfere with the development of this product. A mailing of samples to secretaries of large companies showed a favorable interest. Introduced in 1980, the notes now bring in over $400 million dollars in annual revenue to the 3M corporation.

Don't Bank Your Ideas On Bankers Or Suggestion Programs

If you have had bank managers discard your ideas as whacky, you are not the only one who has learned that you can't bank on your banker liking your ideas. A banker once told Alexander Graham Bell to get out of his bank with "that ridiculous toy". This so called "ridiculous toy" was one of Bell's first models of the telephone.

Getting your banker to think positively about your product may be quite a challenge. In one of my seminar presentations to a banking institution, I used the tandem bicycle from Exercise #6-1 to determine whether its bank managers fully explore ideas; that is evaluate ideas on both positive and negative qualities. Out of about ten comments, there wasn't one positive one. Considering that the bicycle does have some positive attributes, I had to conclude that these bankers were trained to, above all, focus on the negatives. It is no wonder that many good business proposals will receive little financial support from most banks.

> *"When a true genius appears in the world, you will know him by this sign, that all the dunces are in confederacy against him."*
>
> - Jonathan Swift

Incidentally, I also had the opportunity to do a seminar for members of an association who ran suggestion programs for their respective companies. These people didn't fare any better than the bankers; not one positive comment was made about the tandem bicycle. I was amazed that these people who ran suggestion programs didn't know how to fully analyze ideas properly.

Suggestion boxes offer some evidence of the power of people's VOJ. Some companies report that over 50% of their employees' ideas have merit. Toyota claims its Creative Idea Suggestion System has generated over 20,000,000 ideas in 40 years with more than 90% of them accepted.

Other companies report that less than 5% of employees' suggestions have any value. Why the big difference? Surely more than 5% of ideas in any company are useful. In all likelihood, the management of companies which use only a minute number of all ideas submitted are discarding a lot of good ideas. They don't fully explore them for all the positives. They focus on the negatives and discard ideas without any further consideration.

Attack Of The VOJ Idea Killers

"It will never work. It's a dumb idea!" If you have had an idea which was different, chances are you were told it would never work by your colleagues, friends, or family. Practically any successful entrepreneur who has succeeded in developing a radically new service or product has heard this voice-of-judgment idea killer.

"What a great bicycle! Sure beats having him ride me."

Here are just a few of the many VOJ idea killers used to attack an innovative person suggesting something new and different.

- Why hasn't someone else thought of this before?
- Someone else tried something similar and failed.
- It will take a lot of work.
- She has no experience in our industry.
- It will cost too much.
- Top management will never approve it.
- People will think we are crazy.

Treat All Your Ideas To Some PMI

The PMI method is a powerful thinking tool developed by Edward de Bono. It is powerful but yet so simple. Everybody will think they use it all the time; however, a lot of people don't use it at all. In fact, highly intellectual people are more prone than others to not utilize this method because of their confidence in their viewpoint as being the only right one.

The PMI method of thinking is a tool used over a period of a few minutes (two to five) to focus attention on the idea on hand. It is deliberate and is performed in a very disciplined manner to give a more complete exploration of the idea.

PMI is an abbreviation for the types of things that one should consider in the analysis of an idea or a solution to a problem. The letters stand for the following:

- P stands for Plus (positive points)
- M stands for Minus (negative points)
- I stands for Interesting (neutral points)

PMI As An Idea Analyzer

If we were to ask 50 people what they thought about the idea of the government giving everyone $5000 to stimulate the economy, a majority may think it is a good idea. Then, if we asked these same people to reconsider using the PMI method of thinking, we would undoubtedly get some different results. The PMI analysis could look something like this:

PLUS	MINUS	INTERESTING
more spending will result people will be happier more jobs will be created children will leave home	our taxes will go up drug addicts will buy drugs and alcoholics will drink themselves silly more resources will be used up inflation will increase children will leave home	interesting to see how much money is banked interesting to see what people will spend money on interesting to see if charitable donations increase

Note the "INTERESTING" component of the PMI technique has several uses. First, the comments which are neither favorable nor unfavorable can be placed here. Second, the thinker is encouraged to look outside the normal judgmental framework of good or bad. Last, this aspect can lead the thinker to look at another idea by hitchhiking on the one being considered.

When people force themselves to use the PMI method, they usually find that their feelings about the topic change from what they felt at the outset. The final decision can be somewhat of a surprise to themselves. PMI is most useful in those situations where we feel sure about our conclusion from the outset. That is when we need to use this form of analysis the most.

> *"A man with a new idea is a crank until the idea succeeds."*
>
> *- Mark Twain*

Exercise #6-3 - The Advantages (And Disadvantages) Of Drinking On The Job

Assume you run a suggestion program for a large corporation and someone has submitted the following suggestion for increasing productivity:

"I drink only to make my friends seem more interesting."

- Unknown Wise Person

We should allow employees to drink (alcoholic beverages) on the job

Do a PMI analysis on this suggestion to ensure that you fully explore it for its merits. (See Appendix, page 185 for a sample analysis.)

PLUS	MINUS	INTERESTING

Most Organizations Say They Are Innovative - So What?

Let us look at why your innovative ideas and willingness to be highly creative will not find much support in many of today's organizations. This will happen despite the need for organizations to be highly innovative so they can survive and prosper in a competitive global economy. An exercise which is an expanded version of Exercise #1-2 is used here to underscore the way many North American organizations function.

Exercise #6-4 - Only Time Will Tell

Tom Beller, a manager of the marketing department in a large company, is faced with a major problem. The company is attempting to deal with the present business environment which is highly competitive. It is not only constantly changing, but rapidly changing. Constant innovation is necessary to keep ahead of the major competitors.

The immediate problem is with one of the company's best employees, Trina Hamper. She is constantly late for work by about half an hour and shows no sign of improvement. In the manager's opinion, Trina is undoubtedly the department's most valuable employee in the areas of innovation and productivity. She is independent, energetic, and highly creative. The quality of her work is superior to anyone else's. Tom holds her in high esteem and has shown this by rapidly promoting her and giving her more raises than anyone in the company has ever received. In contrast, most of Trina's peers hold her in low esteem and tend to dislike her. So do some of the employees in senior management. She is constantly criticized. Her coming in late is one of several unfavorable things said about her.

> *"Punctuality is the thief of time."*
>
> *- Unknown Wise Person*

Lately, other employees in the company have started coming in late. When confronted about this, they have replied that if Trina can get away with being late, so should they.

What should Tom Beller do to rectify this problem?

Today's most prominent management consultants state that successful companies of the 1990s and beyond will have to fit the following profile:

- Have well trained, creative, and flexible employees
- Provide key employees opportunity for personal growth
- Differentiate their service
- Be quality conscious
- Be lean but extremely responsive
- Be highly innovative

"What luck for rulers that men do not think."

- Adolf Hitler

The case study in Exercise #6-4 represents a situation which, according to participants of my seminars and courses, occurs often in the real world of organizations. (See chapter notes, pages 77 and 78, for potential solutions.) The situation of a highly creative person not being supported has several implications.

Let us look at the qualities or traits highly creative people such as Trina display.

Traits Of Highly-Creative Employees

- Independent
- Persistent
- Highly Motivated And Very Productive
- Risk Takers
- Spontaneous And Strong Sense of Humor
- Use Intuition And Emotions In Decision Making
- Have A Good Balance Between Work And Play
- Have Desire For Privacy
- Can Be Renegades
- Prefer Complex And Asymmetrical Tasks Rather Than The Simple And Symmetrical
- Have Resistance To Indoctrination
- Can Be Hard To Get Along With At Times
- Will Take Stands On Issues
- Relish Disorder And Ambiguity
- Question Things, Especially The Status Quo
- Cause Problems And Don't Care

The most important thing to recognize in the case represented in Exercise #6-4 is the sensitivity of the situation that a manager like Tom Beller has to deal with. It is essential that Trina isn't intimidated into leaving the organization by the manager. He is one of the few supporters she has. This is not uncommon for the highly creative in organizations. In fact, it may be surprising that Tom even supports her. He must have many of the same traits that Trina has.

Many organizations advertise how innovative they are; however, in most cases the word "innovative" is used because it sounds nice. When you look at these organizations, you will see they don't support highly creative people such as Trina who show the initiative to be creative. The question I always pose is: How can companies be truly innovative if they don't support highly creative people?

Most employees, including managers in the higher echelons of organizations, tend to resent stars such as Trina. Middle-of-the-road behavior and mediocre performance are preferred to displays of initiative. When a highly creative individual does step forward to advocate new and innovative ideas, he or she is viewed as a threat and is quite often ostracized by co-workers. Co-workers view him or her as a dangerous competitor who may soon be promoted ahead of them. Many managers will go out of their way to make it difficult for someone who doesn't fit the norm, despite the fact he or she adds immensely to the success and profitability of the organization, much more so than the people who fit the norm.

One of the tools managers have at their disposal to subdue highly creative people is claim they aren't good team players. Team play has been over emphasized lately by the corporate world. Asking people to be team players results in less individualism and less creativity. In many cases managers who stress the importance of being a team player are just looking for yes-men or yes-women to work for them.

> *"If you have a yes-man or yes-woman working for you, one of you is redundant."*
>
> *- Former Xerox Manager*

The individuals with the most potent ideas are the highly creative people who are often renegades. Of course, highly creative people in general aren't good team players. Rather than try to make them team players, managers should support them. The bottom line is ideas don't originate from groups; ideas originate from individuals.

Many managers are looking for a yes-man or yes-woman to work for them because they are threatened by the traits of the highly creative, especially the last four traits listed on page 66. Consequently, insecure managers tend to promote people who aren't highly creative. In a *Fortune* magazine interview (August 31, 1987) Tom Watson, former CEO of then prosperous IBM, had this to say about the type of people he promoted:

> *"I never hesitated to promote someone I didn't like. The comfortable assistant - the nice guy you like to go on fishing trips with - is a great pitfall. Instead I looked for those sharp, scratchy, harsh, almost unpleasant guys who see and tell you about things as they really are. If you can get enough of them around you, and have patience enough to hear them out, there is no limit to where you can go."*

In most large organizations a highly creative person won't be promoted. Someone who acts like an entrepreneur will be relegated or transferred to another position where he or she can no longer practice the entrepreneurial spirit. The organization either tries to tame the person or the employee is fired. Even if he or she isn't forced out, eventually, the highly creative person will realize they won't ever be supported in their creative endeavors, so they leave.

Organizations Need Highly Creative People More Than The Highly Creative Need Organizations

During the present layoffs and buyouts of the corporate downsizing 1990s, which employees do you think agree to voluntarily leave organizations? It's mainly the highly creative. These are the confident, productive risk takers who know they can function without the corporation. They consider corporate life demeaning.

> *"I used up all my sick days so I phoned in dead."*
>
> *- Spotted on T-shirt*

Despite harsh economic conditions, more people than ever are chucking the rigid corporate world for entrepreneurial freedom or to pursue individual interests in areas personally more rewarding than their jobs. Often these "downshifters" end up making less money and working longer hours than they did in corporate life.

Following are the reasons individuals, mainly the highly creative, are leaving the corporate scene in droves.

Reasons Creative People Leave Organizations

- Supervisors taking credit for creative individuals' ideas
- Having to stay the full work day even if the creative worker is twice as productive as someone else and gets the work done way ahead of schedule
- Bureaucracy with red tape, foolish rules, illogical procedures, and unmotivated people specializing in dynamic inaction
- The organization advertising itself as being innovative but not supporting innovative people
- No recognition or acknowledgment for excellence in work
- Working with repulsive yes-men and yes-women who prostitute themselves for salary increases and promotions
- Having to work with jerks and incompetents who should have been fired 10 years ago
- Power struggles within the office involving fierce competition, back stabbing, and paste-on smiles
- Getting less pay than someone who is much less productive but who has been around longer
- Rigid dress codes that stipulate what workers can wear
- No time to just think because of the constant interruptions
- Paperwork - memos that mean nothing and reports no one ever really reads
- No cooperation by other departments
- Double-talk by superiors
- Regular two-hour or longer meetings that go nowhere fast
- Excessive work load
- The organization asking employees not to take full vacation entitlement due to work load
- The organization expecting creative people to take part in social activities with fellow employees who are so socially deprived they have to socialize with people at work
- Overly rigid vacation schedules making it impossible to take vacations at the best times of the year

"Trenton, I am firing you because I can't stand obnoxious yes-men like you."

"Ms. Boles, I couldn't agree with you more. What a brilliant move!"

How Organizations Unsupportive Of Creative People Shoot Themselves In The Foot Three Times

When a highly creative person leaves an organization, the organization is severely affected. Organizations shoot themselves in the foot, not only once or twice, but three times when they allow the highly creative to leave.

- The most obvious effect on organizations is the loss of the services of a highly innovative and productive employee.
- The second effect on the organization is the highly creative individual goes to a competitor much more supportive of creative people. Alternatively, the creative individual becomes the competition by starting a competing organization.
- The third serious effect on the organization, when the creative person leaves, is the remaining employees in the organization have been shown that the organization doesn't support and reward highly creative people. These employees won't see any reason to be more creative.

> *"I don't want any yes-men around me. I want everybody to tell me the truth even if it costs them their jobs."*
>
> *- Samuel Goldwyn*

Corporations such as Hallmark and the 3M Company are known for their support of the highly creative. What have innovative organizations like Hallmark and 3M found out by supporting the highly creative? The highly creative must be allowed to be themselves. They must be given their independence and given shelter. Not only should they be rewarded for success but also for failure. They must be rewarded financially with some incentive for productivity. Highly creative people tend to be very possessive of their ideas and accomplishments; they detest any other employees especially those in higher management taking credit for their achievements. Therefore, these stars must more than anything be given recognition for their achievements.

In regards to creative people, Leon Royer, executive director of organizational learning at 3M, has been quoted: "Either you'll learn to acquire and cultivate them or you'll be eaten alive." Managing the highly creative is definitely not easy; once again my easy rule of life applies. Highly creative individuals have to be considered high maintenance, but they are certainly worth the price.

Why Know-It-Alls Suffer From Specialist's Disease

While working on this book, I received a brochure from an international foundation; the cover states "BE A KNOW-IT-ALL! Here's How". The inside of the brochure states "Join our Foundation and see how easy it is to know it all." I wondered whether these people had thought about the advantages of NOT knowing it all.

There are some real problems with individuals in organizations such as this one who want to be know-it-alls. The biggest problem is that know-it-alls tend to be uncreative. Researchers have found that the more experts, or know-it-alls, think they really "know" something, the less they are open to new approaches. This is called "specialist's disease".

"Know-it-alls" or "experts" in a particular industry may con us into believing that they know more than we do about their industry because they work in that industry. Apparently they are supposed to know what is reasonable and what isn't. Their beliefs can be liabilities. Rigid beliefs and unyielding thinking patterns have been known to stifle creativity in many fields. Elbert Hubbard defined a specialist as "one who limits himself to his chosen mode of ignorance".

In any industry the experts or specialists tend to be the least innovative. There are three things that hinder the creativity of know-it-alls:

> *"No man can be a pure specialist without being in the strict sense an idiot."*
>
> *- George Bernard Shaw*

- Knowledge
- Education
- Experience

Experts suffering from specialist's disease are master idea killers. They think they have all the reasons why something new and different will not work. Consequently, they tend to be the least creative and innovative people in their field. They also tend to be unsupportive of anyone who is trying something innovative.

Specialists will give you a brilliant argument about why things won't work. And they will convince many people along the way because they are great at putting up brilliant arguments. They forget to look at one thing - why it will work!

MBA Doesn't Stand For "Mercedes-Benz Awaiting"

You need to be innovative if you want to be a leader in business today. A Master's in Business Administration (MBA) degree may serve a purpose for many facets of business. However, if you don't have a university or college business degree, you shouldn't feel severely disadvantaged. In fact, you may actually have an advantage over someone with a degree. Business Week magazine recently reported most business programs stifle creativity.

Universities with business programs like the one I attended would like us to believe that MBA stands for "Mercedes-Benz Awaiting". However, as I realized after graduating with a MBA, it doesn't stand for "Mercedes-Benz Awaiting" from creative endeavors. The average MBA graduate is not likely to be highly creative. That is why former Chrysler Chairman Lee Iaccoca said "MBAs know everything and understand nothing." When I went out into the real world, I found out what MBA really stands for. It stands for "Means Bugger All".

These are traits managers should have or things they should be good at if they wish to be successful in today's business world:

> *"You can always tell a Harvard man - but you can't tell him much."*
>
> *- Unknown Wise Person*

- Creativity
- Intuitive decision making
- Vision
- Zest and enthusiasm
- Ability to generate superior customer service

How many management text books used at universities list all these important elements of modern management in the index? Not very many. Peter Drucker was right when he said "When a subject becomes obsolete, universities tend to make it compulsory."

Creativity and innovation in business go beyond having university degrees. The important factors for creative success are factors you will not normally acquire in the school systems. Let's face it, some of the least creative people are individuals with MBA degrees. On the other hand, some of the most creative people in the world of business are individuals who have never heard of an MBA and won't ever need one to keep generating innovative products and services.

Beware Of Specialists Who Aren't So Special

You have just discussed your new idea with the "experts" and they have stated "It won't work". How should you react? You should find out for yourself whether your idea can be a winner. Over the years many individuals with limited knowledge, experience, and education have proved more knowledgeable and experienced experts wrong.

> *"A new idea is delicate. It can be killed by a sneer or a yawn: it can be stabbed to death by a quip and worried to death by a frown on the right man's brow."*
>
> *- Charlie Brower*

Remember that Christopher Columbus went against the belief of the times that the world was flat. Flat-world thinking exists today, only in different forms. There have always been "flat-world thinkers" in all industries. Here are five classic examples:

* Erasmus Wilson, an Oxford University professor, in 1878 said "With regard to the electric light, much has been said for and against it, but I think I may say without contradiction that when the Paris Exhibition closes, electric light will close with it, and no more will be heard of it."

* Charles Duell, Director of the US Patent Office, in 1899 said "Everything that can be invented has been invented."

* Harry Warner, president of Warner Brothers, in 1927 in defence of silent movies said "Who the hell wants to hear actors talk?"

* The United States National Academy of Sciences in 1940 issued a statement declaring that there would never be such a thing as a jet aircraft: "Even considering the improvements possible - the gas turbine could hardly be considered a feasible application to airplanes, mainly because of the difficulty of complying with the stringent weight requirements."

* In 1878 Western Union rejected the exclusive rights to a new invention by stating: "What use could the company make of an electrical toy?" The new invention was the telephone.

My personal experiences have taught me to be wary of someone who tries to impress me with their vast knowledge of their industry based on how long they have been in their occupation. I have found out that often my best bet is to be "unreasonable" and not listen to the "experts." Instead, I find out for myself what can be done and what can't be done in that industry.

After I wrote and published *The Joy Of Not Working*, I received hundreds of letters, the vast majority supportive of the book. One that wasn't all that supportive was from a woman who worked as a free-lance editor. She said that she agreed with a lot of the philosophy of the book; however, the book was badly written and cumbersome to read. This woman was making a proposal to rewrite the book and edit any other books I was thinking of writing.

This specialist editor has two serious problems: One, she is out of touch with reality. Two, she thinks her perception of reality is the only one. Practically everyone else who phoned me, wrote to me, or talked to me in person about *The Joy Of Not Working* stated how well written and easy to read this book was. If I used the editor's services, the book would be written in such a way that the majority of readers wouldn't like it. Of course, she believed her false assumptions that everyone wants to read material which is written in a style more professional than the style I chose. I wasn't about to be taken in by her false assumptions, even though she is an "expert".

It's really easy to get taken in by experts if you aren't paying attention to what's happening around you. Even the so-called best of us can be taken by the experts - and as the following example indicates, it doesn't come cheap.

Remember what happened to NBC about 15 years ago? NBC spent $750,000 (about $2,000,000 in today's dollars) to have some creative specialists develop a new logo. Just as NBC was about to use it, they discovered much to their dismay that the Nebraska Educational Network, a small station in Lincoln, Nebraska, had been using almost the same logo for quite some time. NBC then paid this small station an out-of-court settlement of $55,000 in cash and $500,000 in used television equipment for the right to use this trademark. The total cost to NBC was about $1,305,000 (over $4,000,000 in today's dollars) for the use of this trademark. Oh, by the way - the Lincoln, Nebraska TV station paid about $100 in wages to one of its employees to develop the logo.

Some of the most important discoveries have resulted from people being totally unreasonable and defying the experts. Here are a few examples of people who have succeeded by ignoring the voice of judgment of experts.

* Anita Roddick is the founder of the Body Shop, the largest and most profitable cosmetics company in Great Britain which has also operates in Canada. The company is as well known in Britain and almost as well known in Canada as Coca-Cola and McDonald's are in the USA. Anita Roddick doesn't have an MBA and probably succeeded because she doesn't have one. She says "We survived because we have no rational business knowledge." She succeeded because she didn't know it all.

> *"The guy who invented the first wheel was an idiot. The guy who invented the other three, he was a genius."*
>
> *- Sid Caesar*

* In the late 1980s, two IBM researchers, K. Alex Mueller and J. George Bednorz, disobeyed their bosses and launched a new industry by developing a practical way of creating superconductors. The incredible part of this story is that they weren't experts in this field. They worked with substances that the experts had considered to only have insulating properties and not conductivity potential. By disobeying their superiors and defying the experts, the two men won a Nobel Prize for science.

* Several years ago Jean Pare and Grant Lovig talked to major publishers about getting their first Company's Coming cookbook published. When the publishers weren't as interested in the book as Pare and Lovig would have liked them to be, Pare and Lovig decided to publish the cookbook on their own. Experts in the fields of writing and publishing recommend people don't publish their own books. So how did Lovig and Pare fare not having adhered to this recommendation? Lovig, who had no experience marketing cookbooks, devised creative and unorthodox marketing strategies that the major publishers hadn't used before. The first Company's Coming cookbook sold well over 800,000 copies. This is impressive considering that out of any 55,000 books published annually in North America, only 200 will ever see sales of 200,000 copies, let alone 800,000, in the books' life. Company's Coming now has twelve cookbooks which are Canada's best ever selling series of cookbooks. Over 8,000,000 have been sold to date. Pare and Lovig demonstrated there can be big payoffs from doing something with which the experts don't agree.

The Cure for Specialist's Disease

You will benefit greatly by being able to recognize the people afflicted with "specialist's disease". Learn to ignore people who, while emphasizing their extensive experience, education, and knowledge, try to tell you that you shouldn't try something new in that industry. Follow this principle even if you are an industry newcomer.

"Always listen to experts. They'll tell you what can't be done and why. Then do it!"

- Robert Heinlein

When you undertake a new project, you will discover that many barriers appear out of nowhere. Faced with a barrier to a new project or idea, a person who focuses on experience, education and knowledge will normally stop. The know-it-all person will now have a reason why something can't be done. You must react differently if you want to carry out your idea or project to its completion.

If your strongest trait is a healthy attitude, you are well equipped for giving it your best shot at getting your idea, service, or product successfully implemented. A healthy attitude will serve you in persevering and sticking with your project. With perseverance, you will be well on your way to eventually being a leader of the pack. Whether an idea is ultimately a success or failure, you will be a success because you gave it your best try.

Your next idea will require the same healthy attitude. Sooner or later a winning idea will emerge to make it all worthwhile. You will have left the specialists lurking in the background wondering how you, with less experience and knowledge, were able to pull it off.

Be careful that you yourself don't end up with specialist's disease where your creativity is hindered by knowledge, education, and experience. Am I saying that knowledge, education, and experience aren't valuable for creative endeavors? No! These three can be assets for our creative pursuits provided we build on them and don't use them as a substitute for creativity.

Always be prepared to listen to new ideas whether they come from peers, outsiders, or janitors. Sometimes a janitor will see a solution the highest of executives won't. The cure for specialist's disease is quite simple: Never think of yourself as a specialist. This will allow you to truly profit from the joy of NOT knowing it all.

Chapter Notes

Exercise #6-4

Of course, the first step in solving the problem in this case, as in all problems, is to identify the problem (See page 10). Is Trina the problem or is the organization the problem? In certain organizations, where structure and punctuality are important, Trina could be the problem. The solutions if Trina is the problem focus on motivating her to be on time.

Solutions If Trina Is The Problem

* This solution involves looking at the obvious. Talk to the tardy employee to find out why she is coming in late. Make a request for her to come in on time because of the implications it has to the organization.

* Institute flex-time for everyone, making it okay to be as much as one hour late provided a full eight hours are worked by everyone.

* Offer to drive her to work.

* Make her raise contingent on consistent on-time arrival.

* Serve free coffee and donuts to those there on time.

* Delegate to her the responsibility of making sure that all the other employees are there on time.

* Institute early morning meetings that employees will be embarrassed to miss.

> *"When policy fails, try thinking."*
> *- American Business Maxim*

* Give her the only key to the office with responsibility of opening the office for everyone else including you.

* Fire Trina and hire a less creative person to replace her.

* Change the starting time to half-an-hour later for everyone and see what happens.

* Allow Trina to work on a pet project for one-half day a week if she comes in on time. Pet projects can generate payoffs for the corporation.

* Give Trina an opportunity to attend a seminar at a resort or prestigious location if she comes in on time for the next six months.

Chapter Notes

Exercise #6-4 - (Continued)

In most modern organizations which must be innovative, we would have to consider the organization as the problem rather than Trina. The solutions are much different than if Trina is the problem.

Solutions If The Organization Is The Problem

* Allow her to come in late and explain to everyone else that she has earned it due to her productivity.

* Promote her further and give her executive privilege to come in late.

* Fire everyone else and hire creative employees like Trina to replace the fired ones.

* Change the culture of the organization by giving all employees seminars on the benefits of innovation and how to be more creative. Then give everyone else a chance to be creative.

> *"So much of what we call management consists in making it difficult for people to work."*
>
> *- Peter Drucker*

* Fire Trina and then hire her back as a contract employee who does not come under normal employee regulations. Note, some big corporations in the United States are actually financially and morally supporting some of their top employees to leave the organization and start up their own businesses. The payoff is a partnership with the spin-off companies where both the parent and the infant benefit.

* Allow Trina to work at home for part of the day. Do not extend this privilege to anyone else unless they are as productive as she is.

7. Goaling
For It

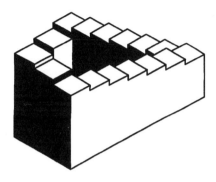

Goaling For What?

If you were to walk in a clockwise direction on the walls of the above figure, you would think you were going up. It would appear to you that you were destined for greater heights. However, in no time you would realize that you are back at the same level that you started. No matter how much energy you put into walking up the steps, higher levels would just be illusions.

> *"It's just as difficult to reach a destination you don't have, as it is to come back from a place you've never been."*
>
> *- Zig Ziglar*

Such is the illusion of activity without well-defined goals. Many people misconstrue their unplanned activity as a direction in life. They wind up putting a lot of energy into these non-goals and end up getting nowhere. Activity is necessary in reaching greater heights, but greater heights only come with defined goals. If we are to arrive at new and worthwhile destinations, we must begin by first defining these destinations. The journey has direction once the destination is set.

"Ever think that self-discovery may lead you to a higher goal than being at lunch five years from now."

The most important point in defining goals is knowing where we want to go or what we want to accomplish. If there is anything that will keep us from getting what we want in life, it is not knowing what we want. Our parents want us to want certain things. Our friends want us to want. Society wants us to want. Advertisers want us to want. These are our non-wants; the question is what do we truly want for ourselves?

Why is it that many of us do not know what we want? We haven't really put much effort into finding out. Where do we want to journey? We can find this out only by taking the time to truly know ourselves. Once we get in touch with our essence, we will know what we want and where we want to go, without needing someone else to tell us what is important to us.

Goal Setting Is Creative, Believe It Or Not!

Is the setting of goals a structuring of activity? Doesn't creativity require unstructured activity? The answer to both of these questions is yes. Remember that creative success is the result of both soft and hard thinking. These two types of thinking respectively translate into unstructured and structured mental activities. By setting goals, we are adding needed structure to our mission of being creative.

Planning is important to innovation. Don't most plans fail? Yes, they do. Someone once remarked that "all plans fail and planning is invaluable". Most plans do not work out exactly the way we want them to. This means a lot of our goals will not be realized in the exact form we define nor within the time frame we set. Nonetheless, goal setting is extremely valuable.

Goals give us something to strive for that we would not otherwise strive for. They give us a purpose. Once we have a purpose and a direction, we have reasons for being innovative and creative. It makes little sense to generate a lot of solutions without a purpose. People tend to be much more creative when they have something to work towards.

Many individuals and organizations become highly creative when a big problem or a disaster arises. They respond in creative ways because there is a need to do so. After Apple Computers became successful with their personal computer, IBM had no choice but to invent one themselves if they wanted to tap some of this lucrative market. The goal was clear: Come up with a new personal computer in a short time frame. IBM responded by setting up a group of managers and designers who worked independently of IBM's central bureaucracy. This allowed the group to work in an environment which was conducive to innovation. The well defined goal was what was needed to motivate IBM's managers and designers to be creative. The result was the highly successful IBM personal computer.

Why Most People Don't "Goal For It"

Researchers say that only about 10% of the population in North America have well defined goals. This may appear surprisingly low for countries which are known for their high achievers. Nonetheless, ten percent of millions of people still translates into a large number of goal seekers. These individuals constitute the minority who are doers. They have direction and make things happen. They set important goals and attain most of them.

> *"Give me a stock clerk with a goal and I will give you a man who will make history. Give me a man without a goal and I will give you a stock clerk."*
>
> *- J. C. Penny*

So how about the rest of the population? What stops the majority from investing the time to define their goals and work towards achieving them? Here are some of the reasons most people do not have goals.

- People are not convinced about the power of goal setting.
- Many people don't know what they want in life.
- Some people don't know how to set goals.
- Embarrassment is a worry for people who are afraid of not reaching their goals.
- Some people have such a low self-image that they don't think they deserve to attain their goals.

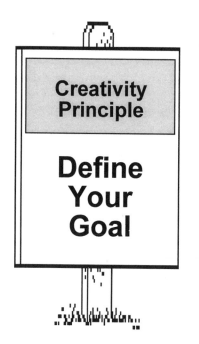

Creativity Principle

Define Your Goal

There is one more reason. Goal setting takes effort and discipline. Once goals have been established, more effort and discipline are required in working towards the goals. Then even more effort and discipline are required to monitor the goals and set new ones. With all the effort and discipline required, many people decide against setting goals and working towards them.

Our daily tabloid newspaper *The Edmonton Sun* carries a scantily dressed lady called Today's Sunshine Girl. The caption for Shona, a recent Sunshine Girl, read *"Fitness Instructor Shona's ambition is to get as far in life as possible - and with form like that we're sure she'll have no trouble at all."*

I personally think if Shona didn't define her goal much better than this, she didn't get very far toward her goal no matter how much most male readers (including me) liked her "form".

Exercise #7-1 - Typical Goals That Don't Work

The following are goals that other people have set for themselves. Which of these are well defined goals?

"I always wanted to be a somebody but I should have been more specific."

- Lily Tomlin

a) To have more money

b) To quit smoking

c) To write a book

d) To be a training specialist

e) To read more books over the next year

Like Shona's goal in life, all of the above goals can be improved upon. Well defined goals should abide by the following principles:

- Goals should be written down.
- Goals should be clearly defined and specific.
- Goals should be realistic, achievable, and measurable.
- Goals should have a target date and a cost limitation.

Last, goals need an action plan to get us going. It tells us what we are going to do to get to where we are going. The action plan defines the type of activity we need to follow in pursuit of our goals.

The Ultimate Goal Is Not A Goal

The ancient sayings on the right bear out the importance of being deeply involved in the process of attaining our goals. The process is more important than the actual goal attainment. Creative people extract more enjoyment and satisfaction from their efforts than from actually reaching their goals. The satisfaction from having reached a goal, no matter how significant, is usually short lived. Many people whose major goal is to be rich are in for a big surprise. A group of New York lottery winners experienced the opposite of what most people expect from a big win. This group formed the Millionaire Circle to deal with what they called "Post-Lottery Depression Syndrome".

> *"All the way to heaven is heaven."*
>
> *- St. Catherine of Siena*

Self-made millionaires tell us that goals as destinations matter less than the process itself. Most successful entrepreneurs state that getting there was most of the fun. Some businesspeople achieve their goal of financial independence and decide to take it easy. Most experience this state for two or three months before they get bored. They then develop new goals to pursue. Entrepreneurs seldom run out of goals because of their constant need for purpose.

Retired people offer more evidence. Many people who finally reach their goal of retirement find that their lives are worse than before. In fact, some retired people don't live very long after leaving the job. They become disenchanted because of their sudden loss of purpose. This absence of purpose is the result of not having more goals to pursue. Successfully retired people are not actually "retired". Retirement is another challenging process.

Robert Louis Stevenson said "To travel hopefully is a better thing than to arrive." Creative people know this. When the ultimate goal becomes the process, life changes. Creativity flows more readily. Failure is viewed as success. Losing means winning. The journey becomes the destination.

> *"The road is better than the inn."*
>
> *- Cervantes*

The Joy Of <u>NOT</u> Working For Someone Else

> *Note: This section is for you if who want to pursue the goal of working for yourself rather than for someone else. The material is adapted from my book The Joy Of Not Working. I am warning you that several people wrote to happily inform me that they quit their jobs after reading the book (although the main theme of the book is to have people enjoy their leisure time like never before). I must issue a disclaimer as I did in the latest printings of The Joy Of Not Working - Any decisions made by you as a result of reading this material is made at your sole responsibility. I assume no legal liability for any decisions made by you after reading this material.*

Despite the high unemployment rate in a prolonged recession, there is a growing wave of people voluntarily defecting from corporations. The dropouts are usually the companies' best performers who feel constrained by corporate life. You may also want to dropout and exercise your own creativity and entrepreneurial skills working for yourself rather than for someone else. By channelling your skills and interests into your own business, you will be developing self-reliance and experiencing self-fulfillment normally stifled in a corporate setting.

> *"One of the symptoms of an approaching nervous breakdown is the belief that one's work is terribly important."*
>
> *- Bertrand Russell*

Working for someone else, especially large organizations, can unbalance your life. Some jobs demand unending attention and won't give you the opportunity to generate the satisfaction you would like in your life. The result is often a miserable you. If you're getting about as much payoff from your job as being the captain of the Titanic, then you must do something to change your state in life.

Here are ten signs you are probably in the wrong job:

* Your main interest in staying in this job is to cope for another 16 years before you can collect a good pension.
* The first hour of work is spent reading the boring sections of yesterday's newspaper.
* You have the record in your organization for the most sick days taken although you are a very healthy person.
* You stay in the shower much too long because you dread going to work every morning except on payday.

* You just don't like this job because you can't express your creative side.
* You are putting off routine things such as visiting friends, paying the bills, and returning phone calls.
* Because you're married to your job, your life is all work and no play.
* You long to be back in university or school even though you didn't like attending either one.
* About 5:00 o'clock on Sunday afternoons your stress level increases dramatically with the thought that tomorrow you will have to go back to work.
* You have nothing good to say about your company even though it recently made it to *The 100 Best Companies To Work For In America.*

We all have a tendency to grow comfortable with existing conditions, even those undesirable to us - there are many forms of mental illness. In the workplace we end up tolerating dead-end jobs, professions we dislike, and companies which mistreat us. The workplace can also be a major source of boredom. A Lou Harris survey found 40 percent of Americans are bored sick with their jobs. We resist making changes because we fear the unknown. I was one of these people while at my engineering job. Reluctant to quit, I stayed on until I was fired. In retrospect, I now see that I subconsciously helped put on the shoe that kicked me out.

> *"The first half of life consists of the capacity to enjoy without the chance, the last half of life consists of the chance without the capacity."*
>
> *- Mark Twain*

The first day your job does not nourish and enthuse you is the day you should consider leaving. Fire yourself if your employer doesn't. Even if you generally like your job, but it takes more than 50 hours a week from your life and you are not pleased with your balance in life, it is time for action. If your spouse calls you a stranger, your kids are on drugs, and you are miserable - why not do something else? My advice is that you QUIT! Forget about these excuses: I can't quit because I need the security; I need to make payments on my big house; I want to send the kids to college; and all the other excuses that arise. Don't wait for the right time. Do it now because there is never a right time; waiting for the right time is another convenient excuse to justify procrastination.

> *"By working faithfully eight hours a day you may eventually get to be boss and work twelve hours a day."*
>
> *- Robert Frost*

No matter how much money you earn, you won't be able to recover the 40 hours or more you are putting into a job that doesn't enliven you. It is impossible for you to buy back enough enjoyment in retirement to make up for what pleasure you missed while working at a lousy job. Ask yourself, "What good is the money going to do if I lose my health?" Many rich people can't buy their health back.

Many people work with the same company until retirement, even if they don't like their job or the company, because they don't want to give up their good salaries. Others, like two school teachers I know, hate what they are doing, but won't change careers because of the generous retirement benefits. Staying in an unpleasant job or undesirable career makes these people function at much less than an optimum level. It also increases their chances of burnout before retirement, so they won't get to enjoy the retirement benefits.

You are imprisoned by the system if you are working just for the money. Don't allow society's idea of financial security to dictate your life. Spending time at a job you hate, just to make money, will interfere with your ability to enjoy life. As odd as it seems, it will also interfere with you making money. There is a common feeling that getting one's financial state in order will help put the individual's other needs in place. The opposite is frequently true. Studies have confirmed that individuals, who satisfy their other needs first by doing what they like doing, generally end up making much more money than individuals who work just for the money in jobs they dislike. It is important to be growing in your job, doing what you like to do, and putting the talents to use that you want to put to use. Attitude jumps back into the picture; if you feel your work is valuable and enjoyable, chances are you will attract enough money to enjoy life.

It's not impossible to leave a job, just difficult. Don't fool yourself by thinking something is impossible, when it is only hard. If you want to do something, and are committed to doing it, you can do it. There is a price to pay, but it will be worth it in the long run. Do your wife a favor, do your kids a favor, do your organization a favor, and do yourself a favor. If you are a school teacher, college instructor, or university professor who dislikes your job, also do society a favor by quitting, since you have no business teaching in the classroom.

If you are considering quitting your job, ask yourself, "What is the worst thing that can happen if I quit my job?" Then to the worst thing that can happen, ask yourself, "So what?" If the downside doesn't involve death or terminal illness, then say the heck with it all. It's not the end of the world. Put things in proper perspective; focus on the positive rather than the negative and life changes dramatically. First of all, you have your health and you are alive. Now think about all the options in your life. In North America, even without a job, you have more opportunity than millions of individuals can ever dream about having on this earth. As for worrying about security, there is no such thing as true security from a job. Knowing you have the ability and creativity to always make a living is the best security you can have.

Once you fire yourself, you may not want another job if you can somehow avoid one without severe financial hardships. Many people feel better about themselves when they quit the corporate life. Even many of those, who do not find something financially rewarding, say they would have a hard time returning to their old corporation.

There will always be some risk in leaving your job; everything worthwhile carries some risk. Besides, you may get fired sooner or later anyway. Remember, with downsizing so prevalent in the 1990s, the odds are increasing that your company will set you free, whether you like it or not (a good sign this is about to happen is when you are given a secretary who is totally illiterate). By voluntarily leaving your job, you get to handle being without a job. You are more proficient at handling the tough situation when it comes up again.

> "Being a housewife and a mother is the biggest job in the world, but if it doesn't interest you, don't do it....... I would have made a terrible mother."
>
> - Katherine Hepburn

The greatest risk may be in NOT leaving your job. If you can't risk being creative and fully alive, what can you risk? Going through the motions in your job means you spend eight to ten hours a day in a boring, joyless, and lackluster way. When your job is taking its toll on your spirit, body, and mind, it is time to get out. There are some things you should not sacrifice for any job. Your dignity and personal worth must come first. If your freedom is at stake, get out of the job. No job is worth the personal sacrifices that will stifle your personal development and interfere with you enjoying life to the fullest.

Here is the complete letter written by a man living in Ontario who decided to go for it after reading the above material in *"The Joy Of Not Working"*.

Dear Ernie:

I have just finished reading your book "The Joy Of Not Working". Your inspirational words have changed the way I now view my life. I always felt that working harder would eliminate my problems, but all it ever did was complicate my life and cause more problems. You have given me the courage to quit my job. I used to be a tax consultant. Now I'm a human being again.

That's right. I marched in this morning and told them I quit because my wife, my kids, and my health (both mental and physical) were more important. I've been seeking security through working more but that's not the answer. There are so many things I've wanted to do but felt I couldn't. I love reading, and I've always felt writing would be a natural extension of my personality. If you have the time, I'd appreciate learning how you got started writing. I also failed first year university English.

Thank You

Les O.

If you last defined your goals sometime ago, they may have changed with time, as did the goals of the gentleman who wrote the above letter. Now may be a good time to review your goals and decide what you want to do with your life.

It is your challenge, and not anyone else's, to find, accept, and develop who you can be as an individual. You must face reality and accept that absolutely everything worth attaining in life - adventure, a relaxed mind, love, spiritual fulfillment, satisfaction, and happiness - has a price. Anything that enhances your existence will take action and effort. If you think otherwise, you will be in for much frustration.

Remember that it is more satisfying to climb mountains than to slide down them sitting on your butt. Sitting around waiting for someone else to light the fire doesn't work. Lighting your own fire, instead of waiting around to be warmed by someone else's, will make this lifetime (and other lifetimes beyond this one if you believe in reincarnation) worth living.

8. In The Land Of The Blind, One Eye Is King

You Can Observe A Lot Just By Watching

It is always interesting to hear what participants in my seminars and courses see in the above figure. Some participants don't see anything. What do you see in it?

A consultant to restaurants in Western Canada makes a good living by saving restaurant operations from having to declare bankruptcy. What does he do that the owners are not able to do? Not much except that he is able to see the obvious. The consultant spots inefficiencies such as too many entrees on the menu. He may also see staff and equipment tied up in unproductive activities.

Creativity Principle

Look For The Obvious

Changes are made that could be recommended by just about anyone except by those directly associated with the restaurant. Many of these restaurants are saved because the obvious problems are pointed out to the owners. Without the consultant, they would not see the obvious and the restaurants would go into receivership.

Many times the best solutions are right before our eyes and we don't see them. The obvious escapes us. Yogi Berra said it well: "You can observe a lot just by watching."

A character in Joseph Heller's *"Catch 22"* had flies in his eyes. He couldn't see these flies in his eyes. Reason: The flies in his eyes prevented him from seeing these same flies in his eyes. Often we are like this character.

Incidentally, there is a bicycle in the previous figure. Once you know it is there, try and not see it. Many things are this way. We won't see the obvious. However, once it is pointed out to us, we can't help but see it.

Exercise #8-1 has an answer which is obvious, yet easy to overlook. Allow yourself 30 seconds to do the exercise.

Exercise #8-1 - Winning By Being The Slowest

A rather eccentric businessman wants to bequeath his financial empire and personal wealth to one of his two sons. He decides that a horse race will be run by the two sons. The son who owns the slower horse will become the owner of everything. Each son fears that the other will cheat by having his horse go slower than it is capable of going. Both of the sons approach a wise old philosopher for his advice. The philosopher, without much delay, tells them in two words how to make sure the race will be fair. What are the two words?

If you are one of the two sons, is there something else you can do to ensure you win the empire?

(See chapter notes, page 98 for solutions.)

Why Didn't I Think Of That?

Following are several examples of creative individuals who have profited from seeing solutions which have many other people saying "Why didn't I think of that?"

* How about starting a newsletter for which the subscribers send you most of the material that you publish? Amy Dacyczyn set aside her career in graphic design to become a mother. In seven years, by saving money rather than earning more, Amy and her husband on an income of less than $30,000 a year still had saved over $49,000 for a house, made major purchases of $38,000, and were completely debt free. They achieved this even though they had four children to support. Thrifty Amy was known as the Frugal Zealot to her friends. Over time she became irked by seemingly intelligent people on daytime talk shows expounding myths such as "Nowadays, a family has to have two incomes to make ends meet." and "Nowadays, families cannot get into the housing market." In June of 1990 Amy started *The Tightwad Gazette,* a newsletter which promotes thrift as a viable alternative life-style. She saw subscriptions climb to over 100,000 in two years. Because Amy doesn't consider her knowledge about thrift to be well rounded, she solicits reader participation. This provides a great source of fresh material to keep her newsletter interesting and loaded with new ideas.

* David Chilton markets information which he labels as "nothing new" in a new way. In the late 1980s Chilton, a stockbroker and financial planner, encountered a problem. He gave his clients various books on financial planning and investing. However, he discovered, much to his disappointment, most clients didn't get around to reading these books. The books all blitzed the readers with boring statistics, graphs, and charts. This is when Chilton decided to write about the basic principles of personal finance and investing in a unique fashion.

> *"The obscure we see eventually. The completely obvious, it seems, takes longer."*
>
> *- Edward R. Murrow*

He took a complex topic and presented it in a reader-friendly way when he wrote *The Wealthy Barber.* Commercial publishers rejected the idea of his book on finance which reads like fiction. So Chilton self-published the book. When he had shown that the book was a hit, a commercial publisher took it over. *The Wealthy Barber* has now sold over 700,000 copies and continues to sell at a torrid rate. Chilton's book, which takes an unconventional approach to a conventional topic, has had many other financial planners saying: "Why didn't I think of that?"

* Robert Plath, a former Northwest Orient pilot, was required to carry more than 40 pounds of manuals with him on every flight. Being a little lazy, he screwed a cart to his carry-on bag. Other pilots figured he was a wimp. Being a wimp - an observant one - had its payoff. Plath invented the Travelpro Rollaboard suitcase with wheels and a retractable handle. Although there were already bag and cart combinations on the market, they didn't look very good to Plath. So he designed his own prototype and had it manufactured in mass quantities in Asia. At first he received a cold response to his invention which the retail market scoffed at. Plath started by selling his units to his former airline colleagues through mail order. In due time retail outlets were begging for his product. It was introduced around 1989 and has had sales of 30 million dollars since then. Industry observers of the luggage industry now call Plath's Rollaboard the biggest invention in more than 15 years.

* In the 1800s bicycle manufacturers overlooked the obvious solution for years. The design of the bicycle first featured two wheels the same size but over time the front wheel got larger and larger. Initially the pedal assembly was attached directly on the front wheel. To make bicycles faster, the front wheel had to be increased in size. The problem was bicycles became rather cumbersome. The solution to this problem was before the industry's eyes. One day someone noticed something that was used in the manufacturing process of bicycles that could be used on the bicycles as well. It was a drive train assembly. This person thought why not use it to power the rear wheel. It was only a matter of time before the bicycle was made with two wheels the same size.

> *"Common sense is not very common."*
>
> *- Latin Proverb*

* Howard Schultz turned an everyday product into a customer craze. Although coffee sales declined since the 1960s due to health concerns, Schultz has elevated Starbucks, the Seattle based gourmet coffee company, into one of the most rapid-growing businesses in North America. In the 1980s Schultz visited Italy on a coffee buying trip and saw the romantic relationship Italians have with coffee. Schultz decided to build a national chain of Starbucks patterned after the Italian coffee bars. He adapted coffee to the American palate by creating offerings such as espresso both straight or diluted. Now it is not uncommon for dedicated customers in places like Seattle and Vancouver to spend $100 a month or more at Starbucks's coffee bars.

Exercises With Obvious Solutions Not So Obvious To Most People

(Solutions to the exercises are in the chapter notes, page 96.)

Exercise #8-2 - Matching Socks In The Dark

Five months ago a man threw away all his old socks and purchased 10 pairs of identical black socks and 4 pairs of identical brown socks. Since then he has lost 3 of the black socks and 1 brown sock. Assume there is a power failure in the evening just as he is about to go out. He is fully dressed except he does not have on his socks and shoes.

> *"Only the most foolish of mice would hide in a cat's ear. But only the wisest of cats would think to look there."*
>
> *- Scott Love*

Unable to see in the darkness of his bedroom, what is the minimum number of socks the man has to remove from his dresser drawer to ensure that he has a matching pair?

Exercise #8-3 - The Obvious On The Typewriter Keyboard

QWERTYUIOP

As you may already know, the above is the top row of the typewriter keyboard. First here is some trivia about the typewriter; the layout of the keyboard was designed in the 1800's to slow typists down because they were jamming up the mechanical keys when typing too fast. We have more efficient keyboards which are compatible to the faster electronic typewriters. People have not accepted the new layouts because of resistance to change, another block to creativity and innovation.

So much for the trivia. What is the longest word that you can make in the English language with the top row of the typewriter keyboard?

Exercise #8-4 - Finding The Fastest Way

As President of Superior Time Air, you have just had a hectic week trying to get a number of projects completed. Time Air has regular scheduled flights to about 20 percent of the cities in Canada and United States. One of the projects involves your Charter Holiday Service. This is a new service just introduced to serve all of North America.

"Common sense in an uncommon degree is what the world calls wisdom."

- Samuel Taylor Coleridge

Your airline has just had 15,000 brochures printed which are slated to be put in travel agencies in all major cities across North America. You are trying to figure the fastest way for you to get these brochures out to all the agents. The peak holiday season is about to start and every minute counts.

Being a creative manager, how are you going to get these brochures to their destinations in the fastest possible time?

Exercise #8-5 - Dressing For Success

A bank in the U.S. realized that it needed to improve its image. One of the problems that needed attention was getting the employees to dress better. The bank was very concerned with what the reaction of the employees would be if a dress code was imposed by senior management. The bank management was able to resolve the problem with little resistance from the employees. What do you think they did?

Exercise #8-6 - Why Aren't They Having Any Fun?

As the new manager of community facilities in a large city, you have noticed that children are not playing in the playgrounds. Someone has told you that children find playgrounds boring. What can you do about this problem?

Exercise #8-7 - The Graffiti Puzzle

Two years ago, while cycling in a residential area I cycle through regularly, I came upon a old Ford truck with the box built up on the sides and a tailgate made from four boards. Painted on the tailgate was some graffiti as indicated on the above drawing.

For the next two weeks I cycled in this area and kept seeing the graffiti on the back of this truck. I figured if this was my truck I would be creative and turn the boards of the tailgate upside down or inside out to make the graffiti unreadable.

However I missed an obvious solution which the owner eventually used to eliminate the graffiti problem. Can you see the obvious solution?

Exercise #8-8   -   Milk It For All You Can

A kid in school was asked by the teacher to name 7 things with milk in them. The boy gave the teacher his answer in 10 seconds. Can you answer this in 10 seconds?

Exercise #8-9   -   Easy To Miss The Boat

A man is sailing in a boat at 10 knots against a wind which is gusting at 5 knots. The man is 38 years old. His boat weighs 98 pounds and he weighs 152 pounds. What nationality is the man?

Chapter Notes

Exercise #8-1

The two words are "Change horses". For the second part of the exercise, you can shoot your horse to make it the slowest.

Exercise #8-2

To get a matching pair, the man only need take out 3 socks.

Exercise #8-3

Don't overlook the obvious. Try the word "typewriter".

Exercise #8-4

As President you should practise a fundamental principle of management: DELEGATE - to the head of the mailroom or the person in charge of these types of tasks.

Exercise #8-5

The new dress code was enthusiastically received by the employees because senior management "gave the problem away". Instead of dictating a policy themselves, management named a committee of employees to come up with a policy. The employees proposed a satisfactory dress code after their research.

Exercise #8-6

Get children involved in the design of your playgrounds.

Exercise #8-7

Hint: Consider the make of truck. If you still can't get it, see Appendix, page 185.

Exercise #8-8

The boy's answer was butter, cheese, ice cream, and 4 cows.

Exercise #8-9

The sailor is Chinese. Why? Okay, the solution is not that obvious but why he is Chinese is very obvious. (See Appendix, page 185.)

9. Thinking Way Out In Left Field

Seeing Double Or Better

As a young lawyer, Abraham Lincoln one day had to plead two similar cases. He happened to get the same Judge for both cases and both cases involved the same principle of law. In the case heard in the morning Lincoln appeared for the Defendant. He made an eloquent plea and easily won his case. Ironically, in the case heard in the afternoon Lincoln happened to be acting for the Plaintiff. Lincoln was arguing this case with the same eagerness only from the opposite point of view when the Judge, somewhat amused, asked Lincoln why he had changed his attitude since the morning. Lincoln replied "Your Honor, I could have been wrong this morning, but I know I'm right this afternoon."

> *"The realization that there are other points of view is the beginning of wisdom."*
>
> *- Charles M. Campbell*

The moral of this true story is don't get stuck in your beliefs. This can come back to haunt you. Structured thinking limits your ability to see things in a different light; instead learn to be a flexible thinker. Go as far as possible to be a divergent thinker on a regular basis.

Most of us have a tendency to structure our thinking patterns in ways which prevent us from seeing all the possibilities there are for finding solutions to life's problems. This tendency has a great impact on our creative abilities.

Test your flexibility in thinking with the following exercise:

Exercise #9-1 - What Is Going On Here?

Betty, a 42 year old school teacher, bought her six year old daughter, Milisa, a new bicycle for her sixth birthday. On this day Milisa was riding the bicycle in front of an office building when she was struck by a car and injured. The police and ambulance were called and both arrived on the scene shortly after. The six year old girl was not injured seriously but the ambulance attendants decided to have her lie down on the stretcher so that she could be taken to the hospital for observation. Just as they were putting the little girl in the ambulance, a 28 year old clerk-typist ran out of the building and screamed "That's Milisa! What happened to my daughter?"

Whose daughter is Milisa, the school teacher's or the clerk-typist's?

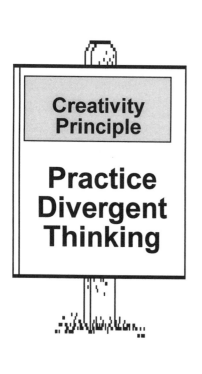

Creativity Principle

Practice Divergent Thinking

To find the most logical solution to Exercise #9-1, most of us require a breaking away from structured thinking patterns. In retrospect the solution is obvious (see chapter notes, page 109). Yet the logical solution escapes many of us due to our set mind patterns.

Flexibility in thinking requires mainly effort on the thinker's part. Researchers have found that most successful people in business have developed the habit of thinking in flexible or non-linear terms. This results in innovative ways of marketing products, financing projects, or managing employees. These people see double or better in business.

Divergent thinking leads to more opportunities for people than does linear or vertical thinking. Lateral thinking, a term coined by Edward de Bono, is another term for divergent thinking. This mode of thinking goes beyond the rational and traditional.

Attempt solving the problem in Exercise #9-2 with lateral thinking.

Exercise #9-2 - The Flag Pole Dilemma

You are the manager of a McDowers hamburger outlet in the United States. McDowers is the largest chain of its kind in the world. Ray Block is the owner and demands excellence from his managers.

The time period is the late sixties. Four days ago a large riot resulted after a demonstration was held at Bent State University. The United States Army was called in to assist state police. In the confusion that resulted, soldiers started shooting and killed four students. Anger and outrage have been expressed all over America, especially in universities and colleges.

> *"A stiff attitude is one of the phenomena of rigor mortis."*
>
> *- Henry S. Haskins*

After listening to the news on the radio, you drive into work and start your day. You work until noon and then take a break. Listening to the news on the radio you hear that marches are being held in all major cites and towns in the states and students are demanding all American flags be flown at half mast. You think about the flag pole in front of your McDowers outlet and the American flag on it. It occurs to you that it is a good thing no marchers are in front of your establishment. Charles Block, your boss, would think it unpatriotic to fly the flag at half mast because of an act the soldiers committed in the line of duty. In fact, you know Mr. Block would fire you if he knew that you bowed to the students' demands and flew your flag at half-mast.

At 2:00 o'clock in the afternoon, your assistant informs you that, a quarter of a mile away, there are 2,000 students on their way to your hamburger outlet demanding that you show your respect for the deceased. They want you to personally go out and lower the flag to half-mast. Television crews and newspaper reporters are accompanying the angry students.

At this point you become very clear that if you do not lower the flag, the students will probably destroy a good part of your building. Charles Block will not be too happy about this. It is likely he will fire you if this happens. On the other hand he will probably fire you if you personally lower the flag since in his opinion this would be unpatriotic.

What will be your course of action?

Exercise #9-3 - Paper Clips For What?

You're the manager of a manufacturing company which by mistake made several million boxes of paper clips for which you have no market. These paper clips are now taking up valuable storage space. What alternatives do you have for disposing of the paper clips?

Exercise #9-2 is based upon a real life situation to which a manager had to react. If your decision was either to lower the flag for the students or to refuse to do so and suffer the consequences of having property damaged, your decision was based on vertical thinking. Divergent thinking was used by the manager who faced this situation in real life (see chapter notes, page 109). His response saved him his job. There are several non-linear solutions to this situation. Can you come up with at least three original ones?

*"This sign works a lot better than **Private Beach, No Swimming**."*

Exercise #9-3 isn't best solved with only linear or vertical thinking. Linear solutions are those which are rational and traditional. One linear solution is to sell the paper clips at the least possible financial loss. Vertical thinking is straight forward thinking which involves careful logical analysis of the solution. Vertical thinkers will think only in terms of getting rid of the paper clips to organizations which want paper clips to clip papers together.

A divergent thinker who attempts Exercise #9-3 will think not only in terms of disposing the paper clips to minimize losses, but also in terms of finding new uses for the paper clips. Divergent thinkers will explore all the different ways of using paper clips rather than just exploring the most logical and promising uses for them. Divergent thinking has to do with new ways of looking at things and generating new ideas of every sort imaginable. In my seminars we do an exercise to show that the uses for paper clips are literally unlimited.

So, remember to move your thoughts from being rigid and focused to a state of being different and interesting. Exercise #9-4 along with the various mind benders provide further practice in divergent thinking. Be sure to look for ideas which stem from the non-linear approach as well as the linear approach.

> *"The art of being wise is the art of knowing what to overlook."*
>
> *- William James*

Exercise #9-4 - Queen Of Stones

Once upon a time, there lived a widowed queen who was selfish, jealous and ugly. She had a beautiful daughter who was loved by a young handsome prince. The princess was in love with the prince as much as the prince was in love with her. They decided to get married but had to get permission from the queen.

The queen also fancied the prince and wanted to marry him. So wealthy was the queen that her garden path was littered with diamonds and rubies. She was willing to give all her wealth to the prince if the prince married her; however, the prince only wanted the princess.

One fine afternoon while the three of them were strolling along the garden path, the queen proposed that they let chance decide who shall marry the prince. She stated that she would choose a ruby and a diamond from the path and put them in a jewelry box. Without looking, the princess would have to pick one of the precious stones from the box. If she chose the diamond the queen would marry the prince and if she chose the ruby the princess would be the lucky one to marry the prince.

The young prince and the princess reluctantly consented to this proposal. As the queen stooped to pick up two stones, the princess noticed that the unscrupulous queen selected two diamonds, instead of a ruby and a diamond, and placed them in the jewelry box. She then asked the princess to choose one of the two stones from the box without looking.

What should the princess do under the circumstances? (See chapter notes, page 109 for solutions.)

Mind Benders To Run Your Mind Off Its Rails

Puzzles force us to think in new ways by challenging the way we think about ideas, numbers, shapes and words. Try these mind benders to practice your divergent thinking. (Solutions are in chapter notes, page 110.)

Mind Bender #1 - Half Of Thirteen Is Not Always 6.5

Use your flexibility in thinking to generate at least seven solutions to "What Is Half Of Thirteen?"

Mind Bender #2 - What Is The Prime Minister Up To?

"A man must have a certain amount of intelligent ignorance to get anywhere."

- Charles F. Kettering

The Prime Minister of Canada has just about completed remodelling the outside of his residence in Ottawa. He still needs something to finish the job. He goes down to the hardware store and looks at some items. If he buys these items, 1 will cost him $2.99 and 10 will cost him $5.98. Based on this he decided to buy 24.

The clerk charged him $5.98. What did the Prime Minister buy?

Mind Bender #3 - Rain, Rain, Don't Need To Go Away

For 35 minutes a 38 year old man walked through a severe rainstorm. He didn't wear a hat, had no umbrella, and didn't hold anything over himself while he was in the rain. Yet he didn't get even one hair on his head wet during these 35 minutes. How was he able to do this?

Mind Bender #4 - The Chicken Or The Egg

A farmer living on the prairies eats four eggs a day for breakfast. He hasn't had any chickens on the farm for two years. He doesn't beg, borrow, steal, or buy the eggs and no one ever gives him anything. Where does the farmer get his eggs?

Mind Bender #5

A child goes to the store with two coins which add up to 30 cents. One of the coins is not a nickel. What are the two coins that the child has?

Mind Bender #6

Seven months of the year have 31 days. How many have 30 days?

Mind Bender #7

Can you think of three different words which become smaller if you add letters to them?

Mind Bender #8

Anthropologists on an excavating expedition were looking for artifacts when one of the junior members excitedly yelled that he had found a gold coin marked 6 B.C. The leader of the expedition took one look at it and said it was not made in 6 B.C. Being one not to tolerate stupidity, the leader fired the junior member on the spot. Why?

Mind Bender #9

A lady is celebrating her 10th birthday. On the same day her daughter who is 20 is getting married. How can this be?

"Great innovators and original thinkers and artists attract the wrath of mediocrities as lightning rods draw the flashes."

- Theodor Reik

Mind Bender #10

A man wants to join five chains, each with four links, into one closed chain. To open a link will cost $1.00 and to close a link will cost $1.50. He was able to create a single closed chain for less than $11.00. How was he able to do this?

Rebus Mind Benders

Here is a whole new batch of rebus exercises I created to help you develop your ability to think divergently. Can you determine what the following rebuses stand for. Example: LVS stands for Elvis.

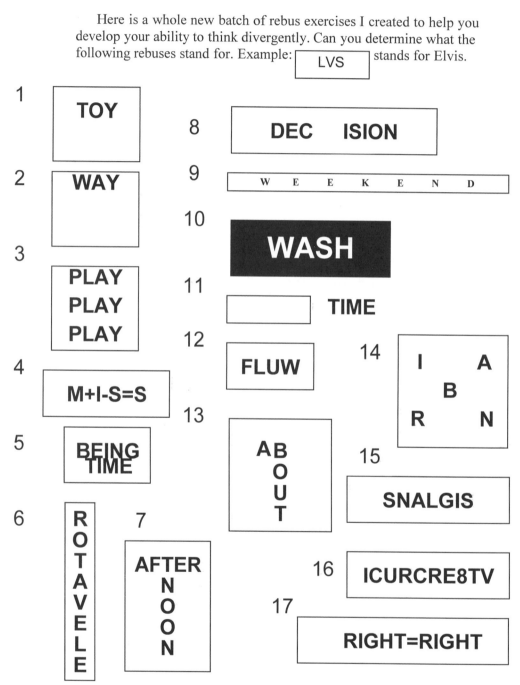

1 TOY

2 WAY

3 PLAY
   PLAY
   PLAY

4 M+I-S=S

5 BEING
   TIME

6 R
   O
   T
   A
   V
   E
   L
   E

7 AFTER
   N
   O
   O
   N

8 DEC ISION

9 W E E K E N D

10 WASH

11 [ ] TIME

12 FLUW

13 A B
    O
    U
    T

14 I   A
       B
    R   N

15 SNALGIS

16 ICURCRE8TV

17 RIGHT=RIGHT

18 **XX XX**

26 **i**

32 **WAYS NO CHARGE!**

19 **SA LARY**

27 To Be Honest

33 **E W E**

20 **ME/THEY ARE**

28 **CIGOL**

21 **BUSINE⌐**

29 MY KNOWLEDGE

22 **SHOOT SHOOT**

30 TIME

34 **SEX≠SEX**

23 **GUN IM**

31 **FAC / TIONS**

35 **DAVID LETTER___**

24 DREAMS

25 blouse SEA

36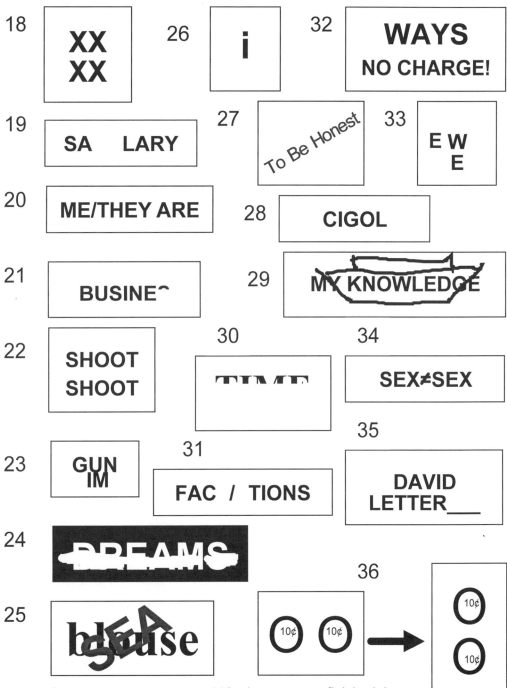

See chapter notes, page 110 when you are finished these.

More Exercises For Divergent Minds

Exercise #9-5

About three years ago the Doonesbury cartoon strip showed a color picture of the USA flag with the main cartoon figure looking at the flag and saying: "Kids here's a real brain-teaser! Try disposing of today's comics section without violating George Bush's proposed constitutional amendment on flag desecration. Sure the flag is only paper, but it's still the US Symbol."

He goes on to say: "No using it to line a bird cage or train a puppy - that's desecration! No throwing it in the garbage and no using it to start a fire in the fireplace - that's flag burning! Good Luck. Then he goes on to say: "Solution? There is none! You're stuck with this flag until it crumbles! Sorry, kids, but that's the way it goes."

I disagree that there is no solution. Can you figure out a solution to this problem? I certainly can. (See chapter notes, page 109 for my solution.)

Exercise #9-6

In 1990, Dick Barr, president of Western Mortgage (Realty) Corp., had a problem with the parking lot in the company's office building on West Broadway in Vancouver. Virtually all the spots were reserved and big signs were posted saying vehicles would be towed away. The problem was people would park in the reserved stalls. By the time a tow truck could be summoned, the culprits had left.

Dick Barr used divergent thinking and came up with an inexpensive solution which reduced most of the illegal parking.

What would you do in a similar situation? (See chapter notes, page 110 for Barr's solution.)

Thinking Way Out In Left Field

Great leaders in business regularly use divergent or non-linear thinking in their decision making. Many experts on management claim that the use or the lack of use of divergent thinking separates successful managers from the less successful ones. Divergent thinking involves being way out in left field.

We all can develop the ability to be more innovative and divergent in our thinking. The payoffs can be big. Here are just a few examples of the payoffs enjoyed as a result of divergent or left-field thinking used by these people in business.

* Canadian Ron Foxcroft spent three years developing a new whistle for referees. He finally perfected his whistle with its distinctive, piercing pitch, but for months after he didn't sell a single whistle in Canada. He said he kept running into typical Canadian negativity and not one sporting-goods store in the many he approached bought a whistle. The owners of one sporting-goods store refused to take the whistle on consignment because it was the dumbest thing they had ever seen.

  Faced with a big problem, Foxcroft resorted to divergent thinking. At the Pan American Games held in Indianapolis, Foxcroft stayed up until the middle of the night and then blew his whistle like never before in the dormitory grounds where 400 referees, judges, and linesmen were sleeping.

  > *"It's them who take advantage that get advantage in this world."*
  >
  > *- George Elliott*

  Foxcroft woke up most of the officials but it paid off. The next day he took orders for 20,000 of his Foxcroft 40 whistle at $6.00 each. Today his whistle is used by lifeguards, snowmobilers, skiers, and officials in every major league except hockey.

* At the age of 28 Jennifer Runyeon bought a bankrupt windshield wiper company which she found advertised in the classifieds. Experts in the automotive industry thought she was foolish to start selling the wipers on television after having raised the price of the wipers from $12.95 to $19.95. Automotive products are normally sold only through retail outlets. Because she had a tight budget, Runyeon promised cable TV stations a percentage of sales rather than payment for the ads. Runyeon's critics were wrong. Her company, Lifetime Products Inc., made $3 million in 1988 and by 1991 the company had racked up sales of $45 million.

107

* In the late 1980s Barry Kukes of Compu-Pak Inc. increased his sales of floppy diskettes 100% in just 5 months to an annual rate of 2 million dollars. How did he do it? By using "new" and "different" packaging. His first hit was the "Swimsuit" floppy diskette which featured a bikini-clad woman on the label. He came up with puppy dog labels and intends to use cars along with some other objects featured in the packaging. Kukes wasn't worried that his packaging did not make any sense. "What does a girl in a swimsuit have to do with a floppy diskette?" you ask. His answer: "We'll be the first to admit, absolutely nothing".

> *"Some fellows get credit for being conservative when they are only stupid."*
>
> *- Kin Hubbard*

* Michael Field's drugstore chain The Medicine Bottle operating in Northern Alberta introduced "Random Acts of Kindness" to the communities the chain serves. Each Medicine Bottle store delivers five bouquets of flowers each week to five people in the community who aren't feeling well. People are invited to submit the name of a relative, friend, or neighbor who is feeling down. Originally a bouquet was to be sent to the first five names submitted, but because of the tremendous response the names are put into a drawbox, from which five are drawn. Because of their community spirit, the staff at The Medicine Bottle received substantial free publicity in local newspapers.

If you want to receive free publicity, remember that the media are not in the business of promoting your product. The people in the media want a good story. Practice divergent thinking. Be first, be daring, and be different and the media will write about you and your business.

* In 1989 Hy's Encore Restaurant in Vancouver was faced with the problem of potential customers thinking that the restaurant was closed. On each side of the restaurant a high-rise building was being demolished making it look like the two-story restaurant building was being demolished as well.

The restaurant took out an advertisement in the Vancouver Sun which showed a picture of Hy's with the buildings being demolished on both sides. The advertisement read:

"Hy's Encore Operating At Full Blast - Despite rumors to the contrary this landmark, amid all the construction activity on Hornby Street, is still open and operating at its 27 year location. Major renovations to the premises are almost complete, providing a stunning new look for customers. Pictured is the first phase of the renovation program which included demolition of adjacent buildings."

Chapter Notes

Exercise #9-1

Note how easy it is for the majority of us to structure our thinking. Although there can be more than one answer to this, the most logical answer is Milisa is the daughter of both the school teacher and the clerk-typist. The clerk-typist happens to be a man married to an older woman. (Only about 20% of seminar participants get this.)

Exercise #9-2

There are many solutions available from lateral thinkers. One of my solutions was to delegate to an assistant manager and get lost. This way I would have some chance of retaining my job by claiming I was not around when the flag was lowered.

The manager who was actually faced with this situation knew that a nearby supplier was about to deliver some food supplies. The manager called the delivery man and told him to hurry over and knock down the flag pole with the delivery truck. The delivery man did this. The manager then phoned his boss and said the flag pole was knocked down by the delivery truck but he would have it back up the next day. He made no mention of the fact he had the flag pole intentionally knocked down.

Exercise #9-3

This exercise is discussed in the Chapter content.

Exercise #9-4

A linear solution is for the princess to choose one stone and sacrifice her happiness. Another is to expose the queen's trickery.

One of the twenty or so good divergent solutions is for the princess to ask the queen to choose a stone and then say that since the queen chose a diamond the one remaining for the princess must be a ruby.

Exercise #9-5

You shouldn't have to be stuck with this flag from the comic strip. Use divergent thinking and send the comic strip depicting the flag to George Bush. If he likes flags so much, he should be happy to get another one even if it is on paper.

Exercise #9-6

Although the parking lot was intended strictly for tenants and not for hourly parkers, Barr posted several big signs advertising parking for $10.00 an hour or portion of an hour. This rate is about five to ten times the normal rate for parking in Vancouver. The outrageous rate helped curb about 75% of the illegal parking that used to occur before the signs were posted. A little problem has arisen; occasionally someone actually comes into the building wanting to pay the $10.00 minimum fee.

Mind Bender #1 - Some solutions are one and three from 1/3, eleven (XI) and two (II) from XI/II, and four from thir/teen.

Mind Bender #2 - Canadians shouldn't need this hint but Americans and other non-Canadians may. The present Prime Minister of Canada is Jean Chretian who is from Quebec. While in office he lives in the official residence at #24 Sussex Drive in the city of Ottawa. Now go back and try the exercise again. (See Appendix, page 185 for solution.)

Mind Bender #3 - The man is bald.

Mind Bender #4 - The farmer eats duck eggs.

Mind Bender #5 - A nickel and a quarter make one of the coins not a nickel.

Mind Bender #6 - 11 (all except February).

Mind Bender #7 - Male, all, mall, small can become smaller. Also pig (piglet).

Mind Bender #8 - A coin marked 6 B.C. doesn't make any sense.

Mind Bender #9 - The lady was born on February 29 and is now 40 years old.

Mind Bender #10 - Open all four links in one of the five chains at a cost of $4.00. Then use these to join together the remaining four chains at a cost of $6.00. Total cost is $10.00.

Rebus Mind Benders - Don't be so lazy. Show some respect and spend a little more time on these. It took me several hours to create these and you want the solutions in a minute or two! (After you have put in some more time trying to solve these, see Appendix, page 185 for the solutions.)

10. Boy Are You Lucky You Have Problems

So What's Your Problem?

How do you view day-to-day problems? Do you always look at a big or complicated problem as an unpleasant situation? Well, you shouldn't. Creative people look at most complex problems as opportunities for growth. Each problem should be welcomed in your life as more opportunity to attain satisfaction. Our greatest satisfaction comes from solving complex problems.

Problems offer great opportunity in our lives, if we want them to. Individuals and corporations will not only survive, but flourish in today's rapidly changing world if they are good problem solvers. Good problem solvers are those who welcome problems and are challenged by them. The challenges start their creative juices flowing. The prescription for success in the modern world is the ability to enjoy and take advantage of problems.

> *"I am an old man and have known a great many troubles, but most of them never happened."*
>
> *- Mark Twain*

Exercise #10-1 - As Easy As Rolling Off A Log

Assume you have a boss who isn't very good with figures. In fact, your boss is the worst person you know when it comes to math. Whenever your boss has a mathematical calculation to do, he comes to see you. Today he wants you to calculate the following equation for him.

$$123 + 456 - 23 = ?$$

Undoubtedly you had no trouble with Exercise #10-1, but how much satisfaction are you experiencing from having solved this problem? Unless you are as bad at math as your fictitious boss, you likely aren't getting any satisfaction at all. Why not? Simply because there wasn't much challenge. If you had a job in which you were required to do elementary math calculations, no matter how high the pay, satisfaction attained would be nil.

Exercise #10-2 - A 5000 Year Old Puzzle To Solve

Now let's assume that your boss also likes puzzles. He is pretty good at puzzles but is stumped by one which he brings to you. This puzzle is about 5000 years old and was developed by the Chinese. Can you solve it?

If:

$$\frac{\overline{}\ \overline{}}{\underline{}} = 6$$

$$\frac{\overline{}}{\overline{}\ \overline{}} = 1$$

$$\frac{\overline{}}{\underline{}} = 3$$

What Does:

$$\frac{\overline{}\ \overline{}}{\underline{}}$$

Represent?

If you solved both exercises, which gave you more satisfaction? Obviously, the second one did. (See chapter notes, page 120 for the solution to the second exercise.) This is a simple manifestation of how increasing the degree of difficulty in problem solving increases the amount of satisfaction.

The point is: The greater the challenge, the more satisfaction that is experienced from solving the problem.

My House Burnt Down And Now I Can See The Moon

Being creative means welcoming problems as opportunities for attaining greater satisfaction in life. The next time you encounter a big problem at work, be conscious of your reactions. If you are self confident, you will experience a good feeling because you have another opportunity to test your creativity. For those of you who feel anxious, remember that you have the ability to be creative and solve problems. Any problem at hand is a great opportunity to generate innovative solutions and extract satisfaction by successfully solving the problem. The Chinese have a proverb which says: "My house burnt down and now I can see the moon." I certainly hope your house or anyone else's doesn't burn down. However, I hope you are able to look at some of your common and not-so-common problems and see some opportunity there.

We all have two choices about problems. The first option is to resist the problem. This is somewhat ineffective. Resistance to problems stems from fear, laziness, or a lack of adequate time. Whatever the reason for the resistance, the problem won't go away. Remember the rule of psychology which states that whatever we resist will persist. This is true with problems. Resistance will ensure the perpetuation of the problem.

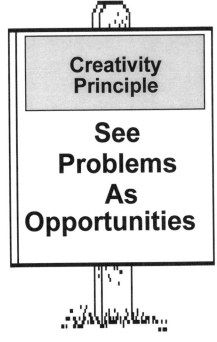

Creativity Principle

See Problems As Opportunities

The second option is for us to do something about the problem. We can draw on our abilities and take control. Highly creative people actually get excited about a new problem because it means a new challenge. The new challenge eventually translates into a heightened state of satisfaction and growth. This occurs when the imminent solution is attained.

The Good, The Bad, And The Ugly Of Problems

"I'll tell you, this whole world has gone bonkers. I was talking to my psychiatrist and he told me his psychiatrist has a lot of problems!"

Many things have been said about problems and how we should handle them. The reality of problems can appear to range from the good to the bad to the ugly. Here are some things to think about. Whether the points are perceived as good, bad, or ugly will depend upon your interpretation.

1. Having a lot of money will not eliminate or reduce our problems. Most people won't believe this despite all the evidence in support of it. People want to believe there is one big money deal in life that will take care of all their problems. This is believing in a form of Santa Claus; everything is going to be great once this saviour brings something of great value for us. Remember how false this belief was when we were children. Our happiness was short lived and our problems remained.

There is much more evidence before our eyes; the newspapers have thousands of stories about rich people who are in trouble with the law or have other major problems. A recent survey showed that a higher percentage of people making over $75,000 a year were dissatisfied with their incomes than of those making less than $75,000 a year. A larger percentage of the rich have alcohol and drug problems than the general population.

I have a theory about how well off we will be with a lot of money. If we are happy and handle problems well when we are making $25,000 a year, we will be happy and handle problems well when we have a lot more money. If we are unhappy and don't handle problems well on $25,000 a year, we can expect the same of ourselves with a lot of money. We will be just as unhappy and handle problems as ineffectively, but with more comfort and style.

2. Successful people in business have more and bigger problems to handle than others less successful. People who have what it takes to make money or run a large company handle and solve problems well. Consequently, they are responsible for more and bigger problems. This is true of chief executive officers. A recent survey in Canadian Business Magazine reported that chief executive officers of Canada's largest corporations work an average of 11 hours a day. Evidently, these CEOs spend a lot of time solving many big problems. Millionaires claim that they still have problems, only more of them.

3. Certain problems can be given away. This is one of the most effective ways to solve problems. I had a problem in negotiating my speaking services because of the time required and because I liked doing other tasks more. This problem is one I gave away. I now have a speaker bureau negotiating on my behalf. If you have a problem with a clerk in a post office who says it is impossible to send your package to a certain destination, the worst thing to do is to complain about the fact it can't be done. The clerk will become defensive and your problem will still be there. Instead give your problem away. Say to the clerk "Now what would you do if you were in my shoes?" By giving your problem to the clerk, you have increased the chances that he or she will find some creative way for getting the package to its destination. If you are a manager, you can give many of your problems away. How? By delegating, of course. Think about problems you can get rid of by giving them to others. Then do it.

> *"There is no such thing as a problem without a gift for you in its hands.*
>
> *You seek problems because you need their gifts."*
>
> *- from Illusions by Richard Bach*

4. When we solve a problem, often it creates more problems. This has many variations. Our problem may be not being married. Once we solve this by getting married, we then get to enjoy all the problems of marriage. Another problem may be our lack of enough clothes. Once solved, we don't have enough closet space and don't know what to wear. A problem of not having enough money when solved with a lottery win leads to many other problems such as old friends not having anything to do with us.

5. Painful incidents or major personal setbacks are often opportunities for creative growth and transformation. Many individuals report that their going through a divorce, or losing the whole wad in Las Vegas, can give the mind a good rattling. The result is an experience of creative awakening. Acts of failure, such as not being promoted, can result in a rebirth of creative thinking which had remained dormant for ages. Some people report that getting fired was the best thing that ever happened to them. Major problems are mind shakers that break old habits of thinking.

6. A problem-free life is probably not worth living. If we were hooked up to a machine which did everything for us, we would eliminate all of our problems. It is likely not one of us will find this as an attractive substitute to life with its inherent problems. Yet, people dream of a problem free life.

> *"Swallow a toad in the morning if you want to encounter nothing more disgusting the rest of the day."*
>
> *- Nicolas Chamfort*

7. If you want to get rid of your problems, just get yourself a bigger problem. Suppose you had a problem of deciding what to do this afternoon. As you were contemplating your dilemma, a big mean grizzly bear started chasing you. The small problem of not knowing what to do will have been eliminated because of the bigger problem of the grizzly. The next time that you have a problem, create a bigger one to get rid of the first one. The smaller problem will be easily forgotten.

8. The best way to enjoy business problems is to be doing a job or running a company we really like. If we want to be master problem solvers, it is terribly important that we love our work. That means we should quit distasteful jobs. The best time to do it is now and we must forget the excuses for staying in situations which we do not relish. Finding work we like means we get to handle problems which we find enjoyable to solve.

9. Most problems can be transformed instantaneously just by changing the context in which we look at them. Why is it that some person can lose all of his millions of dollars and walk away saying "Big deal, it's only money, I still have me." Compare this to another well off person who gets a five dollar parking ticket and loses sleep over it for two nights. The difference is in the context in which the two look at problems.

It isn't the reality or the degree of the problem, but the perceptual choice that determines how we view the seriousness of problems. We can change the quality of our lives just by choosing to change the context in which we view our problems. Context is about whether the glass is half empty or half full. Life works much better when we choose to see the glass as half full.

> *"If all our misfortunes were laid in one common heap whence everyone must take an equal portion, most people would be contented to take their own and depart."*
>
> *- Socrates*

Other Peoples' Problems Can Be Your Opportunities

People have millions of problems. These are our opportunities. The ability to spot and solve other people's problems can enrich our lives. Astute problem spotters and solvers are the movers and shakers in business.

Exercise #10-3 - Focusing On Others' Problems

Identify five problems that others have in personal and business life. Then see if you can come up with some ideas on how to solve these problems by providing new products or services that people will buy.

> *"Visit your mother today. Maybe she hasn't had any problems lately."*
>
> *- Graffiti*

Exercise #10-4 - Your Own Bug List For Fun Or Profit

Think about this: What bugs you? What bugs other people? Choose two "big" bugs and dream up services or products that will help eliminate these bugs.

People Problems Ripe For Business Opportunities

1. Need for cleaner water
2. People unable to enjoy themselves
3. Cities are not friendly places
4. Need to conserve energy resources
5. Older people want to work longer
6. Too many stray dogs and cats
7. Need for creative leisure programs
8. Resort areas are too expensive
9. Schools do not teach creative thinking
10. Businesses want to improve communication
11. Need for more humanistic work
12. Cheaper housing is required
13. Vacant space not rented out
14. Companies are expensive to run
15. Many good products are not marketed effectively
16. Cheaper day care is desired
17. Better quality day care is required
18. Work is too boring
19. How to overcome illiteracy
20. Businesses are going bankrupt
21. How to make people aware of the hunger problem
22. Quality of education is too low
23. Too many young adults are dropping out of schools
24. How to trace children who have disappeared
25. How to make retirement meaningful
26. How to enrich marriages
27. People are lonely
28. How to prevent suicides
29. People need a sense of community in their lives
30. Increase the availability of information
31. Information overload
32. People do not know how to take responsibility
33. People want to make a difference
34. How to improve self-esteem
35. Many products lack quality
36. How to find the right job
37. How to meet new people
38. How to become self-actualized
39. How to spend money prudently
40. How to be happier in life
41. How to have power
42. How to attract funding for community and social programs
43. How to reduce stress
44. How to stay healthy
45. Overly expensive vacations
46. How to deal with nagging relatives and in-laws
47. There are too many choices in life
48. Not enough time to get everything accomplished
49. People are afraid of crime
50. How to enlarge this list to 100 items

"The new year brings 365 days of opportunity."

- Unknown Wise Person

Peoples' Bug List:

Opportunities For New Products And Services

1. Too much news on the radio
2. Having to lick stamps
3. Telephone solicitors
4. Negative people
5. Overly-positive people
6. Cigarette smoke
7. Noisy clocks
8. Too many signs on the streets
9. Potholes on the road
10. Polishing shoes
11. Shaving
12. Terrible books
13. Shoe laces that break
14. Dripping faucets
15. Collection agents
16. Having to take a car to a repair shop
17. Relatives
18. Insecure show-off yuppies
19. Burnt out light bulbs
20. Having to buy a Christmas tree
21. Newspapers with negative news
22. Having to write letters
23. Not knowing what to write in letters
24. Boredom with life
25. Government red tape
26. Big bunches of keys
27. Yappy dogs
28. Bad service in retail outlets
29. Products that don't work
30. Cars parked in front of your house
31. Dents on your car when in parking lots

32. People taking up two parking stalls
33. People who drive too fast
34. Soap dishes that you can't get the soap out of
35. Having to write an essay, article, book, resume, etc.
36. Two for one pizza of which even one isn't worth eating
37. Shoe heels that wear out
38. Shoes that never feel broken in
39. One good stocking left
40. Junk mail
41. Small bathtubs
42. Mowing lawns
43. Noisy parties next door
44. Having to wait in line ups
45. Members of the opposite sex who come on too strong

> *"I shall make electricity so cheap that only the rich can afford to burn candles."*
>
> - Thomas Edison

46. Too much advertising on T.V. and in magazines
47. Offensive TV commercials
48. Cafeteria food tasting like paper
49. Having to deal with obnoxious people
50. Long lists like this one

Big Problems, Big Opportunities

When it comes to problems, we must remember that the bigger the problem, the bigger the opportunity. Here is an example:

Bette Nesmith Graham had a big problem. She worked as a typist but made many typing errors. Bette knew that other typists had the same problem. Because of this, she founded a multi-million dollar industry. In the early fifties, IBM introduced their new electric typewriters with carbon film ribbons. When typists tried to erase typographical errors, a terrible mess was left behind on the paper. To overcome this problem Bette developed a white paint to use in correcting her typos. The paint worked well. She called it *"Liquid Paper"*. When Bette Graham offered IBM her new product, she was turned down. This problem was also an opportunity. She decided to market Liquid Paper herself. When Bette died in 1980, she was worth 50 million dollars.

A problem customer is another example of an opportunity - the more vocal the customer, the bigger the opportunity. The successful handling of the problem can translate into some free advertising. If you can handle the irate customer's complaints to his or her satisfaction, he or she will become loyal to your business. Anyone this vocal will tell a lot of people about your organization and be a great source of word-of-mouth advertising.

> *"If you keep your head when all about you are losing theirs - you don't understand the problem."*
>
> *- Unknown*

Our careers or businesses depend on individuals' problems. All of our work involves some sort of problem solving. People will always have problems; we will always have many opportunities for solving these problems. Focusing on problems can make us rich and famous (if that is what we want). Even more important than wealth and fame is the satisfaction and enjoyment that comes from our effective solving of problems.

Chapter Notes

Exercise #10-2

The answer is 4. By looking at the first three sets of three lines we can determine a pattern. The first line of the three represents 1, the second represents 2, and the third represents 4. If any of these lines is broken, then the line represents zero. The sum of the three lines represents the number. Therefore the one in question is:

$$0 + 0 + 4 = 4$$

11. How To Be A Successful Failure

To Be More Successful, Fail A Lot More

Exercise #11-1 - Name This Man

Twice this person failed in business. He ran for State Legislature and didn't make it. Two times he lost in his bid for Congress. He did no better in the Senate races; twice he was defeated. Success eluded him when he worked hard to become Vice President of the United States. The woman he loved died when she was very young. Eventually this man suffered a nervous breakdown.

Who was this man?

Exercise #11-2   - The Key To Business Success

What is the most important quality, above all else, which chief executives and entrepreneurs have that helps them achieve their success?

Creativity Principle

Take Risks

The last chapter stressed that problems are opportunities and the bigger the problem to solve, the greater satisfaction we will obtain from solving that problem. If this is the case, why do many people avoid certain problems more than they would avoid a pit-bull terrier with rabies? One of the biggest reasons is fear of failure.

Many people avoid the risk of failure not realizing that success usually comes after a lot of failure. Take the example of the man in Exercise #11-1. This man was none other than Abraham Lincoln. All his "failure" happened before he became one of the most famous Presidents of the United States.

On one hand, North American society is obsessed with attaining success. On the other hand, most people are afraid of failure and try to avoid it. The need for success and the desire to avoid failure are contradictory. Failure is just a necessary step to success. Often you will have to experience many failures before you experience success. The road to success looks something like this:

Failure Failure Failure Failure Failure Failure Failure Failure Failure SUCCESS

"A lot of disappointed people have been left standing on the street corner waiting for the bus marked Perfection."

- Donald Kennedy

The road to success is paved with failure - failure and nothing else. Yet many people attempt to avoid failure at all costs. Fear of failure is associated with other fears such as fear of being seen as a fool, fear of being criticized, fear of losing the respect of the group, and fear of losing financial security. Avoiding failure means avoiding success. You have to fail a lot to attain success. Of course, the way to double your success rate is to double your failure rate.

Afraid Of Being A Fool Is Foolish

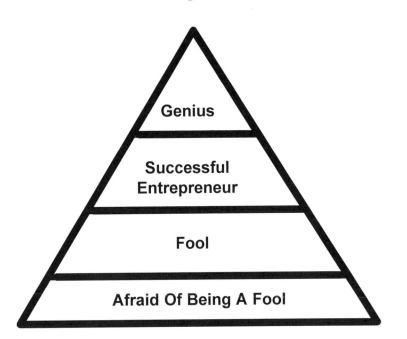

Participants in my seminars cite "the fear of failure" as a creativity barrier or bandit; however, I point out to them that it isn't the fear of failure so much as the fear of what others will think about us. Many of us avoid taking risks because of our fear of looking bad if we fail. We get so obsessed with being liked that we won't do things which we feel may make us look bad in the eyes of others. Avoidance of risk becomes the norm. This is detrimental not only to our creativity but to our liveliness as well. We must learn to be fools if we are to be creative and live life to the fullest.

> *"There is a thin line between genius and insanity. I have erased that line."*
>
> *- Oscar Levant*

Many of us believe there is a hierarchy in life as shown above. On top are the geniuses. Then come the successful entrepreneurs who never fail. If we take a hard look at the apparent geniuses of the world, we find that genius is nothing more than perseverance and persistence disguised. Einstein and Edison had many successes but they also had an incredible number of failures.

There is level worse than being a fool: "Afraid of being a fool" is much worse than being a fool. Geniuses, effective leaders, and successful entrepreneurs have handled the fear of being a fool. They realize that in order to succeed in their endeavors they have to first be a fool; being foolish is essential to life's mastery. The point is that being "a fool" is on a much higher plane than being "afraid of being a fool" is. Life requires that we be fools now and then.

If you worry a lot about what others will think about you, I have some important news for you: Researchers indicate that on a good day 80 percent of all individuals' thoughts are negative. Just think what percentage this is on a bad day. It looks like most people are going to have bad thoughts about you anyway. That is what most individuals' thinking is all about. So what difference does it make? The heck with what others think! You may as well go for it!

Try Celebrating Your Failures

Successful entrepreneurs and managers are good at taking risks. Seldom do they take outrageous risks. The risks they take are normally calculated to be reasonable so that the chances of winning are not so small as to be a stupid gamble and not so large as to be a sure thing. Today's leaders give themselves challenges which represent a reasonable probability of loss and a reasonable probability of gain.

Let's return to Exercise #11-2. There are many important factors for the success of entrepreneurs and managers. These include communication, vision, leadership, integrity, sensitivity, flexibility in thinking, confidence, courage, and constructive nonconformity. But the Centre for Creative Leadership in Greensboro, North Carolina found there is one factor that stands out more than the others. This is what gives achievers the final edge.

The biggest factor is their ability to manage failure. Successful people aren't hindered or stopped by failure. They look at failure differently. They learn from it; they actually welcome and celebrate failure.

Setbacks Experienced By Successful People

With risk comes the probability of failure. That's the price we must be prepared to accept. The greater the risks, the greater the probability of loss. However, with greater risks come bigger payoffs. Here are some examples of people who have succeeded despite their initial failures in life.

> *"The worst part of success is trying to find someone who is happy for you."*
>
> *- Bette Midler*

* Today Diane Sawyer has one of the best jobs in television news. She is the network newscaster for Prime Time Live. However Sawyer paid her dues working as a weather reporter in Louisville, Kentucky for three years.

* Actor (and comedian) Robin Williams was voted least likely to succeed by his classmates.

* Before Christie Brinkley became a supermodel in the 1970s and 1980s, she had a tendency to be overweight and admitted she was "a self-conscious teenager who was chubby with chipmunk cheeks".

* Jay Leno, host of the Tonight Show, once worked as an opening act in a brothel.

* John Grisham, author of *The Firm* and *The Client* which have sold millions of copies, had his first novel (*A Time To Kill*) rejected by 28 publishers. When Wynwood Press undertook *A Time To Kill*, it sold only 5000 copies.

* Michael Jordon didn't make his high school basketball team in his second year because he wasn't good enough (or so said his coach).

* Television personality Phil Donahue starting working in a bank after he failed his first audition as a radio broadcaster.

* Matthew Coon Come, grand chief of the Quebec Cree Indians, has had many setbacks battling Hydro-Quebec, trying to protect his peoples' land from flooding and river diversions. However, through his creative ways to bring attention to this matter and his victories in Canadian courts, he has prompted the cancellation of lucrative Hydro-Quebec export contracts. Recently Coon Come won one of the world's prestigious environmental awards, the $60,000 prize from the Goldman Environmental Foundation.

* Jane Pauley is now a winner as a famous television personality on The Today Show but she was a six-time loser in the Homecoming Queen elections at her school.

Exercise #11-3: What do these people have in common?

- Lee Iaccoca (Former CEO of Chrysler)
- Sally Jessy Raphael (Television talk-show host)
- Rush Limbaugh (Radio talk-show host)
- Lily Tomlin (Actress and comedian)
- David Letterman (Television talk-show host)
- Stephen Jobs (founder of Apple Computers)
- Ernie Zelinski

> *"To rebel in season is not to rebel."*
>
> *- Greek Proverb*

I bet most of you wanted to say what all the above people have in common is they're all famous; however, my name on the list destroyed that thought. Actually, the answer is all the above people were fired from their jobs at one time or another.

Lee Iaccoca was fired from Ford Motor Company despite his great accomplishments there before he was hired by Chrysler. Henry Ford III told Iaccoca he was being fired simply because Ford didn't like Iaccoca. Rush Limbaugh, the popular radio broadcaster, claims he was fired from all but two of the jobs he ever had. Stephen Jobs was fired from Apple Computers, the company he cofounded. Sally Jessy Raphael was fired eighteen times in thirty-six years in the broadcasting business.

David Letterman was fired from a job as a weatherman on an Indianapolis TV station for jokingly reporting hailstones the size of "canned hams." Lily Tomlin was fired from a Howard Johnson's restaurant for announcing on the PA system "Your favorite waitress Lily Tomlin is about to make her appearance on the floor. Let's give her a big hand." Customers were amused but not management.

Why was I fired? At the utility company, for which I had worked six years, I took 8 weeks of deserved vacation which my superiors didn't want me to take. I enjoyed the vacation but the management didn't. I was given a permanent vacation when I returned to work. But I am in pretty good company with Limbaugh, Raphael, Iaccoca, Tomlin, Jobs, and Letterman. Can you say this? If you haven't been fired from a job, you aren't being overly creative.

Warning: Success Often Leads To Failure

"Positive thinkers" want us to believe that success almost always leads to more success. There is some truth to success helping create more success. It builds confidence in individuals and organizations. In addition, many new techniques and principles are learned on the way to success. These usually help attain future success.

> *"Someone who tries to do something and fails is a lot better off than the person who tries to do nothing and succeeds."*
>
> *- Unknown Wise Person*

What "positive thinkers" often don't point out is nothing breeds failure like success. More often than is acknowledged, success leads to failure. There are two major reasons for this. The first one is the law of averages. Normally we have more unsuccessful endeavors than successful ones. The odds for failure are much greater than for success, even just after being successful.

The second reason for success leading to failure relates to ego and complacency. Organizations and individuals who make it big usually get fat heads. They tend to think they have the solution and now they know it all. Nothing can be further from the truth. No matter how successful a product, service, or technique is, it won't be the right one for all circumstances. As we know, circumstances have a tendency to change. When circumstances change abruptly, many organizations and individuals are faced with a product, service, or technique which no longer serves its purpose well. The organization or individual isn't able to adequately respond to the new business climate. Tough times follow.

Entrepreneurs have been known to build highly successful companies and then find themselves in deep financial trouble. What sometimes happens is entrepreneurs, men more so than women, want to show the world they have arrived. They buy a big house, an expensive car, and a host of other items. Money is siphoned out of the business just when the business becomes highly successful. The problem is that competitors usually move in when they see a business making it big in a certain industry. This is when the successful business requires a large amount of money to deal with the competition. If it doesn't have the money, the once successful company soon finds itself in deep financial trouble. Success then leads to failure.

You Can't Make A Difference By Being The Same

Exercise #11-4 - A Common Trait In Uncommon People

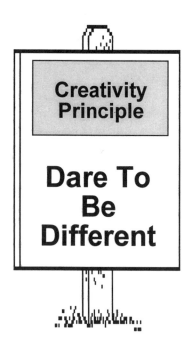

Creativity Principle

Dare To Be Different

What did the following people have in common?

- Mother Teresa
- Thomas Edison
- Albert Einstein
- John F. Kennedy
- Gandhi
- Nelson Mandela

What is the best way to make a big difference in this world? Answer: *Start off by being different.* Being creative is thinking something different. It is also being different than most people. We must diverge from the norm to generate something new and worthwhile. This will take courage, since people who diverge from the norm are frowned upon. We must dare to be different if we are to achieve something important.

Don't let the urge to be nice to everyone interfere with your being different. Having the urge to be nice to everyone translates into wanting to be liked by everyone. Robin Chandler, a British actor, states "The disease of niceness cripples more lives than alcoholism. Nice people are simply afraid to say no, are constantly worrying about what others think of them, constantly adapting their behavior to please - never getting to do what they want to do."

"Don't play for safety. It's the most dangerous game in the world."

- Sir Hugh Walpole

If you want your life to be interesting and exciting, be different. Be different than you normally are and be different than the majority of people in your life. One warning must be given here. You won't get much support from your friends, co-workers, or society when you take the step to be different. They certainly won't encourage you to stand out.

128

Your motivation to be different has to come from within. The motivation should come from the realization that anything of major consequence in this world was probably initiated by someone who was different than the rest of society. In fact they were probably out of step with society to a large degree.

> *"Two roads diverged in a wood and I took the one less travelled by, and that has made all the difference."*
>
> *- Robert Frost*

Just think about the individuals in Exercise #11-4. Thomas Edison, Albert Einstein, Mother Teresa, Ghandi, John F. Kennedy, and Nelson Mandela made a big difference. What they have in common is that they are or were different than the majority. They were out of step; none of these people were conformists.

The point is that being an achiever means being different and feeling good about it. Some people may be uncomfortable with you and others may dislike you for it. You will be criticized a lot. The more success you have at being different, the more you may be disliked. But people will respect you for it, especially when you start making that big difference. You will also have your own respect.

Exercise #11-5

Write down how you are limiting yourself in your life by trying to be like everyone else so that you fit in and are accepted. What can you do to be different that will help you make a difference? What will the consequences be?

> *"I would rather sit on a pumpkin, and have it all to myself, than be crowded on a velvet cushion."*
>
> *- Henry David Thoreau*

Rules And Assumptions Not To Be Ruled By

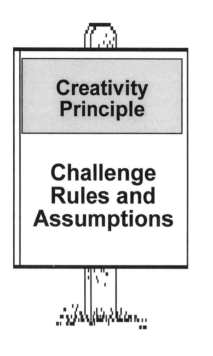

Creativity Principle

Challenge Rules and Assumptions

Being different means challenging the status quo. It is a good idea for individuals and organizations to constantly challenge rules and assumptions. Discarding outmoded rules and unproven assumptions throws a new perspective on business situations. Innovation tends to flow freer and the performance of organizations improves.

Many rules, both written and unwritten, are outdated and serve absolutely no purpose. Often rules are followed without any thought to whether there is a purpose for them. Rules can hinder the generation of new ideas and impede implementation of innovative ways of doing business.

For many years Canadian doctors and lawyers subjected themselves to a rule that restricted the advertising of their services. This rule interfered with their ability to tell the public about their being in business and the types of services they have to offer. Only after constant challenging of this rule by their members have these professionals come to grips with the obsolescence of the rule. Now more advertising is allowed.

We should constantly challenge not only rules but also assumptions. Our voices of judgment constantly make assumptions about the way things are. Often these assumptions have little or no relationship to the ways things are. Only through challenging of assumptions can we determine their validity.

For example, most managers still erroneously assume money is the prime motivator of employees. If managers make the wrong assumption that all employees are motivated by money, they will be ineffective in motivating employees. Researchers have found that recognition and room for growth are better motivators than money. Money as the prime motivator is only one of many wrong assumptions being made which hinder organizational effectiveness.

Breaking The Rules For Fun And Profit

Many businesses owe their success to their willingness to challenge prevailing assumptions and rules of their industry. Because most businesses in all industries don't have the presence of mind to challenge the status quo, a great deal of opportunity exists for the businesses and individuals who develop new methods by challenging the rules. If we look at any of today's highly-successful businesses, we will see businesses which are risking, being different, and challenging the rules.

> *"There ain't no rules around here. We're trying to accomplish something."*
>
> *- Thomas Edison*

Following are a few examples of individuals and businesses which have profited from their willingness to challenge old ways of doing business.

* Anita Roddick's Body Shop chain of stores mentioned in Chapter 6 has been known to break many rules: The Body Shop doesn't spend money on advertising in an industry which spends hundreds of millions on marketing and advertising. The Body Shop relies strictly on word of mouth. The Body Shop doesn't spend much money on research as do most cosmetic companies. What is the main tool for its research? Nothing more than a suggestion box for customers placed in each store. In the cosmetics industry packaging and image are important, or so say the experts. The Body Shop uses refillable bottles initially designed for somewhat of a different purpose - for collecting urine specimens. Roddick encourages each store to commit 25% (not .25% like many companies) of its profits to a community project. Post cards are used to print their annual reports.

* Steven Nichols went in the opposite direction and broke the rules by which Nike and Reebok play in the multi-million dollar sneaker business. For the big companies the average shelf life for sneaker models is four months. These companies base sales strategy on having ever changing trendy models for fickle teenagers. Nichols with his K-Swiss Company has taken his sales from $20 million in 1986 to $150 million in 1993 by selling models that aren't discontinued to a more mature market of weekend athletes and tennis enthusiasts. Many retailers like his sneakers because they don't have to constantly discount discontinued models and replace them with trendy models.

* To differentiate his company's cough syrup from the competition, Frank Buckley decided to risk and break a rule of advertising which states you should not focus on the negatives of your product. W.K. Buckley Ltd.'s cough mixture was invented 70 years ago. It tasted awful at the time and still tastes awful. In the mid-1980s Buckley's Mixture sales had fallen to 4% of market share for cough syrups. Defying conventional marketing wisdom, Frank Buckley decided to emphasize Buckleys Mixture's bad taste in the product's promotional campaign. For example, a transit ad featured Frank Buckley's sour face with ad copy "I wake up with nightmares that someone is giving me a taste of my own medicine." Buckley's advertising campaign's won several awards. The cough mixture's sales increased 16% in 1989 when industry sales declined 1%, and market share rose to 6%.

Ya Gotta Break The Rules When Ya Speak

The presenter paced frantically. He put his hands in his pockets. He yelled. He swore. He didn't dress as well as he could have. I discussed this speaker's performance with the 1989-1990 International President of Toastmasters. He observed this speaker broke every rule of Toastmasters except one. The rule this speaker didn't break: Connect with your audience.

> *"I would tell myself I was about to address the largest mass assembly of idiots ever gathered in the history of mankind."*
>
> *- Winston Churchill's reply to how he prepared for his speeches*

Whether you are a university student or a chief executive officer, you will probably have to make a presentation before a group at one time or another. My advice is if you want to make an effective speech, learn the rules of speaking, and then break as many of them as you can.

The speaker cited above was Tom Peters, coauthor of *In Search Of Excellence* and several other bestselling books. He didn't follow the rules, yet he drew over 1500 people to his Vancouver performance. His annual income from speaking engagements reportedly runs into the millions.

One reason Tom Peters does so well is he is a creative person. Being creative in any endeavor means challenging and sometimes breaking both written and unwritten rules. Rules relate to process and we often concentrate too much on following the right process instead of getting the right results.

Anyone who has read a book or taken a course on how to make effective presentations has encountered many rules for doing things right. A lot of these are perfectly valid - as guidelines. Taken as commandments, they can actually hurt your performance.

Here are seven rules commonly propounded by people who specialize in teaching us how to make good presentations. Some I break regularly myself without anyone seeming to suffer. The rest I have seen other speakers break to their advantage.

Rule - Know Exactly What You Are Going To Say. It is important to have a basic plan for any speech or presentation. But sticking entirely to your planned presentation can rob you of the opportunity to discover something new. In seminars and university lectures, I often leave open a section of my presentation for "winging it". Some of the most valuable planned activities I now use were discovered spontaneously when I tried something new.

Rule - Take A Break After An Hour. Ninety minutes into a recent three-hour presentation on creativity, I asked the participants if they wanted a break. They suggested that we continue and take our coffee on the run. We never did take an official break during that session, and the ratings were excellent - so much for the rule about the break. The point is that if you have generated a high energy level, you don't have to kill the momentum half way through the presentation because the clock strikes 10:00 AM. Breaks are for the participants' benefit; take one when it will benefit the participants.

> *"Most people can tire of a lecture in ten minutes; clever people can do it in five. Sensible people never go to lectures at all."*
>
> *- Stephen Leacock*

Rule - Allow Discussion But Not Arguments. The purpose of this rule apparently is to eliminate unpleasantness. Yes, heated debates are distasteful to some people, but others enjoy them. "I like sessions which get my adrenaline flowing" read the comment on the seminar evaluation form that first prompted me to start breaking the "no arguments" rule. I now encourage heated debates. More people appear to enjoy this than be put off by it. Yes, vigorous arguments have to be managed properly, but they can make a session far more engaging to most participants.

Rule - Allow Time For Questions. This indeed may be an ironclad rule if you're responsible for training people. But if you're essentially just delivering a speech? A few of the best-paid speakers admit that they avoid questions because they aren't good at answering them. Avoiding questions doesn't seem to hurt them. These speakers remain highly popular; they get hired again and again. If you want to avoid questions, see if you can get away with it. If your audience likes your presentation, you will have no problem.

Rule - Use Visuals. At an international conference a few months ago, an expert on critical thinking spoke for one and a half hours without using a single visual aid. His presentation was one of the best I have ever heard. I also saw a presenter who didn't move from the overhead projector for his entire 90-minute presentation. If not awful, he was mediocre at best. A lot of speakers (I am one of them) make a rule always to use some visuals. I don't believe everyone has to.

> *"He charged nothing for his preaching and it was worth it too."*
>
> *- Mark Twain*

Rule - Don't Get Upset And If You Do Don't Show It. The North American advice industry possesses a somewhat peculiar belief there is something intrinsically wrong with a speaker getting angry or highly emotional. I do not share this belief. If I have a good reason, I don't hold back. I let the audience know I how I feel. What benefit can result from being emotional in front of people? Getting upset show the participants that I care. If I care, they care as well.

Rule - Don't Make Fun Of Anyone. I can make fun of certain characters and have everyone in the session happy. When someone obviously is looking for attention in my sessions, I pick on this person. To this type of character, negative attention is better than none at all. The person is happy to get the attention. The rest of the participants are happy to see me pick on the "jerk". Of course, I am happy to have all the participants happy. Note that you shouldn't poke fun at just anyone for the sake of ridicule alone.

> *"When both a speaker and an audience are confused, the speech is profound."*
>
> *- Oscar Wilde*

As a public speaker, the only rule you shouldn't break is to connect with your audience. If you're doing everything else by the book, but failing to connect, it's time you threw away the rule book. Try breaking some of those rules for a change.

12. Creative Thinking Is An Exercise In Silliness

Kilroy was not here!
- *Clem*

Growing Up May Be Harmful To Your Health

The above figure is one of the mysterious "Clem" who originated in Britain and has appeared in thousands of washrooms across many nations. He has been mistaken for the legendary "Kilroy was here" which originated in United States and has also had great washroom presence. Over the years Kilroy's name has been combined with Clem's picture in North American washrooms. Most North Americans think Clem is Kilroy. Not so. Clem is Clem and Kilroy is Kilroy.

"Imagination was given to man to compensate him for what he is not. A sense of humor was provided to console him for what he is."

- Horace Walpole, Man of Letters

By now you are probably wondering what this story has to do with this book. Absolutely nothing. I just kind of like the story and I needed a creative way to get your attention for this section. I thought this would be a good time to be silly and unreasonable. Besides I always wanted to tell people this trivia about Clem and Kilroy that is of absolutely no use to anyone.

Creativity Principle

Have Fun And Be Foolish

Oscar Wilde said "Life is much too important to be taken seriously". How serious are you in life? Do you find time to laugh, play, and be foolish? If you are always serious and trying to be reasonable, you are sabotaging your creativity. Individuals who are too serious to have fun rarely come up with something new and stunning.

Play is at the heart of creativity. Playing and having fun are great ways to stimulate our minds. When we are having fun, we tend to be relaxed and enthusiastic. Sometimes we even let go and become outrageous. All of these states complement the creative spirit.

Hundreds of thousands of people in their 60s, 70s, 80s, and 90s have an incredible zest for life and show great vigor, enthusiasm, and physical ability in living. To some seniors, being over the hill means picking up speed. Seniors who live life to the fullest have this enlightened awareness about how much alive they really are. They have developed certain character traits which really stand out.

Exercise #12-1 - Who Needs A Second Childhood?

Spend two or three minutes thinking about individuals who are in their 60s or older and are still vibrant, active, and enjoying life to the fullest. List the qualities which these people have.

One of the most precious traits which seniors with a zest for life have is their continuing wonder with life - the ability to enjoy each new rainbow, sunset, and full moon. Here are some other qualities that participants in my seminars list for the vibrant seniors they know:

- creative
- spontaneous
- sense of humor
- playful
- energetic
- friendly
- inquisitive
- laughing
- crazy
- ability to act foolish
- adventurous
- joyful

> *"You don't stop laughing because you grow old, you grow old because you stop laughing."*
>
> *- Michael Pritchard*

Exercise #12-2 - Who Else Qualifies?

What age group other than that of seniors has most or all of the above qualities?

The qualities are those that children possess. In other words, people who are active and happy in their later years don't need a second childhood because they never gave up their first. Ever wonder why children are so creative? One of the important reasons is they know how to play and have fun. Remember when you were a child. When you were playing, you were learning. You probably learned a lot more during your lighter moments than during your serious moments. Try and re-experience the child in you if you want to increase your creativity.

Creativity requires playfulness, daydreaming, and foolishness. These are things society discourages. We are told to "grow up". We must be able to ignore what the majority in society wants us to be like. For us to be more innovative, we must learn new ways of playing with things, words, puzzles, ideas, and other people. We must never grow up. Why? When we grow up, we stop growing.

> *"When I grow up, I want to be a little boy."*
>
> *- Joseph Heller*

Humor Is No Laughing Matter

In his early 90s George Burns started taking bookings for his 100th birthday. If he lives for more than a century, it will probably be because of the attitude he has carried through life. He has made a living out of humor. Undoubtedly, his health has benefited from his work. Researchers are finding that boisterous laughing many times a day will give you the same effects as a ten-mile run. Another man who benefited from laughter was Norman Cousins. Faced with what doctors diagnosed as a terminal illness, Cousins proved the medics wrong by watching reruns of Candid Camera and Groucho Marx films. He was able to laugh himself back to health.

Besides being good for our health, humor is an effective way to promote creativity. Experts in creativity have observed that stunning solutions are often triggered by humor. Seriousness hinders the creative flow. When you are under a lot of stress or stuck in a serious state of mind, the best thing is to get out a joke book. Get together with someone who can laugh about anything. Fool around. You'll be surprised at the number of creative ideas that start to flow.

Several years ago a group of high school students were given a test in creativity. Two equal sub-groups were formed. One of the sub-groups enjoyed the half hour before the test by listening to a recording of a comedian. The other sub-group spent the half-hour in silence. When subjected to the test, the students in the first group did much better than the second group.

> *"A light heart lives long."*
>
> *- Shakespeare*

Comedy and laughing will open up your thinking. Laughing tends to make you look at things in unusual ways. This is because laughter changes your state of mind. There is little concern for being wrong or being practical. It is okay to be foolish. This fosters the flow of creative solutions.

Poking fun at work situations is one way to stimulate creativity. You are more apt to break the rules when poking fun at a problem. In a state of playing with the problem your defences are down and your mental locks released. This results in more innovative and exciting responses to the problem at hand. Managers should learn how to encourage their employees to poke fun at all important matters in the workplace.

Exercise #12-3 - Abbreviations To Elongate Your Mind

Why not have some fun before your next important office meeting? Fun puts everyone in a better state of mind. One way is to play some game or do puzzles. The abbreviations below stand for relationships and associations of which you should be aware. Have fun with these before you make up your own. Then give them to your colleagues to figure out before your next meeting.

Examples:

24H. = 1D. (24 Hours = 1 Day) N.N. = G.N. (No News = Good News)

1. 4 P. = E.
2. B.M.W. + M.B. + P. + J. = F. C.
3. 12 I. = 1 F.
4. S. + W. + E. + N. = 4 D.
5. S.C. resides at the N.P.
6. 50 S. = U.S.A.
7. 10 D. = 1 C.
8. 1 + 3 Z. = 1 T.
9. L.A. + S.F. + S.D. are in C.
10. J. F. K. + R. N. + R. R. were P.
11. I. W. T. H. Y. H. was sung by the B.
12. a P.S. = a P.E.
13. W.G.U.M.C.D.
14. 1 Y. + 1 D. = 11 Y.
15. M. J. sings with the R. S.
16. H. + W. + C. = F.
17. J. C. was born on C. D.
18. I.C., I.S., I.C.
19. S. + 2 D. = M.
20. W.P. + N.Y.T + W.S.J + U.S.T = N.
21. J. + P. + R. + G. = T. B.
22. a L.Y. + 4 Y. = a L.Y.
23. E.J. + R.S. + M. + M.J. = S.
24. C.P. + J.F.K.I.A. are in N.Y.
25. 24 M. = 2 Y.

> "Seriousness is the only refuge of the shallow."
>
> - Oscar Wilde

(See Appendix, page 186 for solution to 1 and hints to the others.)

More Graffiti To Cleanse Your Mind

With all the barriers to creativity in our society, many people find that the only place they get to be creative is in the washroom. A lot of the graffiti they write is highly creative. Here are two more pages of it. Please share these with your fellow workers before your next meeting. Your group's creativity may be opened up.

GOD IS DEAD

(Our God is alive; sorry to hear about yours)

58% of all deaths are fatal

There is a dance in this town every Saturday Night this week

What will you do when Jesus comes?
(Move Gretzky to right wing)

There is no such thing as Gravity. The earth sucks.

Lassie kills chickens

JESUS SAVES!
Even more than the Superstore?

The world ends at 10 tonight— —details on the 11:00 o'clock news

Mary had a little lamb and boy was she surprised

I bet you I could stop gambling

Dionne Quintuplets were a hoax - Five couples were charged in the conspiracy

An empty taxi stopped and Ronald Reagan got out

Orville was right

I'm not prejudiced. I hate everyone equally

TIME IS NATURE'S WAY OF KEEPING EVERYTHING FROM HAPPENING AT ONCE

Can a blue man sing the whites?

Snoopy has fleas

The hangman lets us down

My inferiority complexes are not as good as yours

I wrote on this wall because it was here

140

Twiggy is only skin deep

Alimony is like buying hay
for a dead cow.

Mona Lisa was framed

Chicken Man has a Fowl mouth

If you do it in a MG, don't
boast about your Triumphs

*You're never alone with
schizophrenia*

Perforation is a rip off

Roget's Thesaurus dominates,
regulates, rules, OK, all right,
adequately.

GOD LOVES YOU
(God won't love you for
destroying someone's property by
writing on it.)

Dyslexia lures, KO

**Ben Johnson gave
us the runaround**

WET PAINT
(This is not an instruction)

Hypochondria is the one
disease that I don't have.

I love grils
(which was corrected thus:)

You mean girls stupid!
(but then corrected again)

What about us grils?

Arrange the following words
into a well-known phrase or
saying:
OFF PISS

I never used to be able to
finish anything, but now I.......

This wall will shortly be
available in paperback

Clairvoyance Is Dead
I knew you were going to
write this

Absolute zero is cool

Repeal the banana

Kilroy Was Here!
I was not.
- signed Kilroy

Putting Humor To Serious Use

Here is an example of how humor helped me market my books and seminars. After publishing my first book I wound up with about 25 defective books which were either cut crooked or had missing pages. I took these back to my printer expecting a refund. However, the printer told me he had given me 80 extra copies over and above those I paid for. Since I didn't want to throw these defective copies away, I decided to hang on to them for a while.

> *"If an idea does not appear bizarre, there is no hope for it."*
>
> *- Niels Bohr, Physicist*

One day I ran into Lance B., a former colleague of mine. We decided to go have coffee since Lance wanted to talk about how I had published the book. In our discussion I mentioned that I had some defective books which I was trying to put to good use. Lance jokingly said something silly like "send them to people whom you don't like." When someone says something silly or foolish, I have an urge to do better. So I responded by saying "I can do better than that; I can cut these books in half and mail either a top half or bottom half to people."

That night when I went home and retired for the night, I couldn't sleep because I hadn't followed one of my important principles of creativity: Write down all ideas. I got out of bed and wrote "cut books in half and send to people" in my little black book. A week later I was trying to decide how to get companies more interested in my book and seminars. I didn't want to send any more free books since the response was not all that good. I happened to look in my black book and saw "cut books in half and send to people."

This is exactly what I did. First, I went down to my printer and had him cut the books in half. Then, I drafted the letter shown on the next page. Of course my voice of judgment jumped in and tried to convince me this was a "dumb idea" which wouldn't work and wouldn't be good for my image. However after some PMI analysis, I decided to be unreasonable and do it anyway. Sure, I knew some people would think I was crazy or unprofessional. But I also knew a lot of people would remember me. In addition, my curiosity was getting the best of me; I was wondering how people would respond to receiving either a top or bottom half of my book. I felt a little silly while stuffing half-books in envelopes. In the end, this silly and mischievous promotion was well worth the effort.

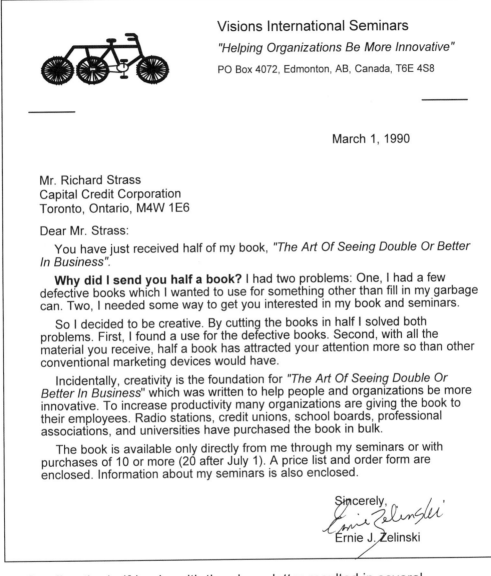

Visions International Seminars

"Helping Organizations Be More Innovative"

PO Box 4072, Edmonton, AB, Canada, T6E 4S8

March 1, 1990

Mr. Richard Strass
Capital Credit Corporation
Toronto, Ontario, M4W 1E6

Dear Mr. Strass:

You have just received half of my book, *"The Art Of Seeing Double Or Better In Business"*.

Why did I send you half a book? I had two problems: One, I had a few defective books which I wanted to use for something other than fill in my garbage can. Two, I needed some way to get you interested in my book and seminars.

So I decided to be creative. By cutting the books in half I solved both problems. First, I found a use for the defective books. Second, with all the material you receive, half a book has attracted your attention more so than other conventional marketing devices would have.

Incidentally, creativity is the foundation for *"The Art Of Seeing Double Or Better In Business"* which was written to help people and organizations be more innovative. To increase productivity many organizations are giving the book to their employees. Radio stations, credit unions, school boards, professional associations, and universities have purchased the book in bulk.

The book is available only directly from me through my seminars or with purchases of 10 or more (20 after July 1). A price list and order form are enclosed. Information about my seminars is also enclosed.

Sincerely,

Ernie J. Zelinski

Sending the half-books with the above letter resulted in several orders for 10 books which further led to sales of 200 books as well as several seminar presentations for one client. The extra revenues totalled between $10,000 and $20,000. I also received a lot of valuable publicity via newspaper articles. In fact, considering the profits this generated, I found out I can cut perfectly good books in half and still have this type of promotion be very profitable.

There Is Reason To Be Unreasonable

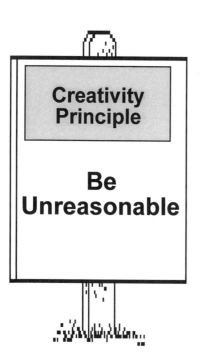

Creativity Principle

Be Unreasonable

Society and our educational institutions teach us to be reasonable and practical. Being reasonable and practical is a fine alternative if we are talking about not doing something stupid like jumping off a cliff. The problem is that society wants us to be "reasonable" in ways which hinder our creativity.

Just because the majority in society holds a belief, the belief isn't necessarily true. What society considers reasonable may actually be very unreasonable. Many people have held false beliefs before. Remember that nearly all of humankind at one time thought the world was flat. This point made by Bertrand Russell offers much food for thought.

"The fact that an opinion has been widely held is no evidence whatever that it is not entirely absurd; indeed in view of the silliness of the majority of mankind, a widespread belief is more likely to be foolish than sensible."

Another philosopher, Albert Einstein, stated "Great spirits have always encountered violent opposition from mediocre minds". When we are considering something new and different, we don't have to look far to have someone tell us we are being unreasonable. We must be on guard and reject reason. Following the reason of others has wrecked many individuals' plans.

"Nothing is ever accomplished by a reasonable man."

- American Proverb

If we are to create anything that makes a difference in this world, we must also learn to challenge our own reasonableness. Remember that our own voices of judgment can be an enemy of our plans. Our own reasons for not doing something should constantly be challenged if we are to succeed in our creative endeavors.

I personally have found that "being unreasonable" is something that can be done on a daily basis. When I encounter either my own voice of judgment or someone else's, I try to go against the prevailing reason. By being unreasonable, I find some surprising and rewarding events occur.

> *"There is no great genius without a mixture of madness."*
>
> *- Aristotle*

One time I decided to be unreasonable and go talk to a Professor who had given me a much lower mark than I thought I deserved on a mid-term paper. What made my going to see him unreasonable was that at least four other students in his class felt the same way about their marks and had already gone to see him. He became very defensive and refused to give any of them any consideration for a higher mark. My unreasonableness paid off. I was able to get consideration from him despite four other students having tried before me. I just did things a little differently. I did not make him wrong by saying that he graded my paper unfairly. Instead I said to him "I messed up my last paper which means I won't get a good final mark in this course. This will cost me an assistantship worth $3000. What would you do if you were in my shoes?" He responded by reducing the weight of the mid-term paper and putting more weight on the final. I wound up with honors and my $3000.

Smart Minds Ask Dumb Questions

We regularly condition our houses, we regularly condition our cars, we regularly condition our bicycles, some of us even regularly condition our bodies, but few of us regularly condition our minds. Regularly conditioning our minds can be as beneficial as regularly conditioning our bodies. Many people are in great physical condition, but their minds aren't in equally great condition. The ability to think critically and creatively is a rarely developed ability.

As children, we asked many dumb questions. We were curious and saw much wonder in this world. As adults, we can continue to challenge our minds with the new and mysterious. We should ask at least one dumb question a day. There can be much wonder until the day we die. We don't know everything there is to know (although a lot of us think we do). In fact, dumb minds have an answer for everything, while smart minds regularly ask dumb questions.

With so many interesting things about which we can think and ask questions, there is no reason for our minds to become rusty. If you can't generate your own mysteries to contemplate at this moment, here are four to get you started:

1. Why do we drive on a parkway and park on a driveway?
2. Why are your toes in front of and not behind your feet?
3. Why does a cow stand still while the farmer burglarizes it?
4. Why is this question in itself a dumb question?

One of the best ways to practice being unreasonable is to ask random "what if" questions. These are questions that may sound absurd and unreasonable. Nonetheless, "what if's" can lead us to some interesting notions. Here are some examples of "what if" questions:

* <u>What if</u> we marketed our product with something unrelated?
* <u>What if</u> we invited our top customers to our Christmas party?
* <u>What if</u> we asked our employees to buy competitors' products?

<u>Benefits Of "What If" Questions</u>

- First, we get the opportunity to explore certain possibilities that we would not otherwise do.
- Second, "what if" questions may lead us to ideas altogether different from the one we started with.
- Last, "what if" questions are a lot of fun.

"I'm not an answering machine, I'm a questioning machine. If we have all the answers, how come we're in such a mess."

- Douglas Cardinal, Architect

A creative mind is an active mind, and an active mind asks many questions. Only through active questioning can we keep our minds developing and discovering new ways of thinking. Questioning our values, questioning our beliefs, and questioning why we are doing things the way we are doing them should be normal. Socrates, a great thinker in his time, encouraged his students to question everything, including what he was teaching them. You should use your mind in active ways to ensure you aren't letting it rust away. You must use it or lose it!

146

13. Zen
There Was
The Now

Don't Be At The Bus Depot When Your Ship Comes In

Exercise #13-1 - The Three Secrets To Fulfillment

A North American entrepreneur had acquired a lot of material wealth but still wasn't happy in life. He heard about a Zen master living in the far east on a mountain hard to find. This Zen master knew three important secrets about how to live life to the fullest. The entrepreneur heard that anyone who had found out these three secrets and had followed them ended up living a happy, fulfilling life.

Because his life was so empty and often dejecting, the entrepreneur decided to go in search of this Zen master. He felt he needed to know what the three secrets were so he could start living life to the fullest. After twenty months of searching, the entrepreneur finally found this Zen master high on top of an obscure mountain.

The Zen master was happy to reveal the three secrets to having a happy and satisfying life. The entrepreneur was surprised at what he was told. What do you think the three secrets were? (For the three secrets, see the Appendix, page 186.)

> *"The best way to make your dreams come true is to wake up."*
>
> *- Paul Valery*

Creativity Principle

Be In The Now

At a Safeway store I frequent there are two express cashouts with one of the cashout counters being closer to the exit than the other one. Long ago I became fascinated by the number of people who are in a hurry, yet are totally unconscious about the fastest way to get out of the store. Many customers will get in the lineup that has the most people. This lineup looks more appealing because the cashout counter is closer to the exit of the building. These people don't pay attention. They fail to see that the second express, which is next to the first one but farther from the exit, will be faster because there are anywhere from one to five fewer people in it.

Some philosopher once said that 95% of the people are unconscious 95% of the time. After seeing many situations similar to the above one in the Safeway store, I wonder if this person isn't right. I will venture to say that this is the cause of most of the misery in the world.

It appears to me that most people aren't in the present moment very often. This is very unfortunate since they miss out on many opportunities in life. Of course, the fact they are this way is somewhat fortunate for people who choose to be conscious. For example, I get in the short line in Safeway and am well on my merry way while others, who arrived at the checkouts ahead of me, are waiting impatiently for their line to move.

"All my possessions for one moment of time."

- Queen Elizabeth I

Having presence of mind or paying attention to the moment is something most of us can improve upon and benefit from. Those of us who don't pay attention are the ones who wind up at the bus depot when our ships come in. The ability to be in the now and concentrate on the task at hand is a very important aspect of the creative process.

Mastering The Moment

Being in the now is nothing more than enjoying the present for all it's worth. This is what Mij Relge, a very good friend of mine, has been able to do. At the age of 43, Mij quit his job as a university professor to do some soul searching, and grow as a person. Out of curiosity, I asked him what he was doing with all his free time, and what his plans were for the future. This was after he had been jobless for about two years. Mij responded with a Zen-type answer indicating he wasn't having any trouble at all with his work-free life. He replied that he was simply "mastering the moment."

Being in the now is emphasized in Zen, an Eastern discipline, which has personal enlightenment as its goal. The following Zen story illustrates the importance of mastering the moment:

A student of Zen asked his teacher, "Master, what is Zen?" The master replied, "Zen is sweeping the floors when you sweep the floors, eating when you eat, and sleeping when you sleep." The student responded by saying, "Master that is so simple." "Of course" said the Master. "But so few people ever do it."

Most people are seldom in the present moment. This is unfortunate since they miss out on many opportunities in life. Having presence of mind, or paying attention to the moment, is something upon which most of us can improve, and from which we all can benefit. The ability to be in the now and concentrate on the task at hand is a very important aspect of the creative process for both work and play.

"Must be nice to cruise around in a Porsche."

"Must be nice to just goof off for the afternoon."

Essential to your mastering the moment is learning to do one thing at a time, instead of two or three. Doing something physically and thinking about something else at the same time are contradictory. You aren't free to take part in your chosen activity if you are thinking about something else. One of the problems we have with leisure is choosing something and sticking with it until it is time to quit. Any act or task should be worthy of our total attention, if it is worth doing at all.

Test your ability to experience and live the now by doing the following exercise:

Exercise #13-2 - Contemplating A Paper Clip

Choose a simple object like a piece of chalk or a paper clip. Concentrate on the object for five minutes. Your task is not to let any other thoughts interfere with your thoughts about the object. In thinking about the object, think about the form as well as the concept behind the form. Where did the object come from? Who invented it? Why is it shaped the way it is?

Here is another good test for how well you can enjoy the moment: When taking a shower, try to eliminate all your thoughts about everything in your life. When you can get to a point where all you are experiencing is the pleasant and relaxing sound of the water running, you are truly experiencing a shower. When you try this, you will notice how easy it is to think about other things, many of which rob you of energy and the moment.

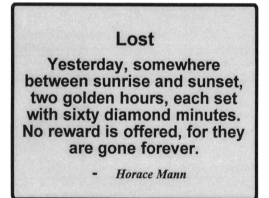

Lost

Yesterday, somewhere between sunrise and sunset, two golden hours, each set with sixty diamond minutes. No reward is offered, for they are gone forever.

- *Horace Mann*

If you didn't do what was suggested in Exercise #13-2 and instead kept on reading, you have shown how you are driven by your old self. So stop now. Go back and do the exercise! If you aren't able to do it, forget about being able to truly master the moment, and just be. You are driven by external forces which will continue to dominate the way you react.

If you did get around to doing Exercise #13-2, how did you do? If you are like most people, you had trouble with wandering thoughts. You became critical, judgmental, or helpless in doing and thinking about this ridiculous exercise. Having difficulty with this exercise indicates how your thinking is very much out of control. You don't have to despair. Practice can help you overcome this. You can develop the ability to be in the here and now, if you want to.

The following three exercises will help you develop your ability to be in the here and now. Individuals who have used these exercises report improvement in their ability to enjoy the moment.

Exercise #13-3 - Concentrating On Concentration

Take a simple object and study it intently for 5 minutes every day. Concentrate on its form, as well as the form behind it. After two or three days, when you have totally explored the first object, use another simple object. Change objects as necessary. This exercise should be done for at least 30 days straight. The gestation period is this long, because this is how long it takes for our minds to change and develop better concentration. Every time you miss a day, you should go back to square one and try for 30 days straight. The benefits of this exercise cannot be explained in normal engineering or business school logic. Nevertheless, the benefits are real. Your subconscious faculties will open up to enable you to concentrate in ways you haven't concentrated before.

Exercise #13-4 - Clocking Your Concentration

Have the alarm of your clock or watch go off at various times of the day to remind you to be in the here and now, so you can enjoy the moment. Use this as a reminder to have the presence of mind to get totally immersed in what you are doing. This can be a reminder to truly enjoy your work by doing one thing at a time. It may be a reminder to appreciate the

> *"For fast-acting relief, try slowing down."*
>
> *- Lily Tomlin*

taste of food by eating slowly. You may be reminded to fully experience a beautiful sunset, or to be totally present with the people around you. No matter what it is, try and do what you are doing completely, instead of doing it in a mediocre way while your mind is thousands of miles away.

Exercise #13-5 - Control of Emotions

This exercise can be practised at any time and at any place. The purpose is to concentrate on your emotional feelings, anytime they occur. Whenever your emotions - positive or negative - are aroused, try to be aware of the reasons for them. Ask yourself what message the feelings are conveying. Why are you feeling this way? Do your feelings have to do with worry, fear, anxiety, or guilt?

Although this exercise seems to interfere with our spontaneity, it does just the opposite. This exercise helps us to get in tune with the messages from inside. In turn, we are better able to act upon what we feel without repressing any feelings. Spontaneity, which is discussed later, is actually increased when we improve our presence of mind.

The ability to experience the here and now is a characteristic of creatively alive individuals. Creatively alive people are those who can get totally immersed in a project. Their concentration level is so high that they lose all sense of time. Their project totally envelopes them - having distracting thoughts isn't a problem. Their secret? They enjoy the moment for what it is, and don't worry about what is coming up next.

Ultimately Nothing Matters And So What If It Did?

> *"It is only possible to live happily ever after on a day to day basis."*
>
> *- Margaret Bonnano*

Worrying about the trivial or important is one of the activities which robs people of the now. About 15 percent of the US public spends at least 50 percent of each day worrying says a study from Pennsylvania State University. Worry is so rampant in North America that certain researchers claim approximately one out of three people in North American society has serious mental problems as a result of worrying.

To put worrying in proper perspective, the following story is another one told in Zen teachings:

The Muddy Road - A Zen Story

Two monks, Eanzan and Tekido, were walking along a muddy road when they came upon a beautiful woman unable to cross the road without getting her silk shoes muddy. Without saying a word, Eanzan picked up and carried the woman across the road, leaving her on the other side. Then the two monks continued walking without talking until the end of the day. When they reached their destination, Tekido said, "You know monks are to avoid women. Why did you pick up that woman this morning?" Eanzan replied, "I left her on the side of the road this morning. Why are you at this time still carrying her?"

The above story emphasizes the Zen philosophy about the importance of going through life not carrying around problems from the past. Yet many people focus on former problems. Worrying comprises most of people's thinking, with some people so addicted to worry, that they worry if they don't have anything to worry about.

Exercise #13-6 - Two Days About Which Not To Worry

There are two days of the week about which you should not worry. What are these two days?

Fear, anxiety, and guilt are emotions related to worrying. At any given time, at work or elsewhere, people's minds are far, far away - mostly thinking about worries and regrets. Most people are worrying about what happened yesterday or what will happen tomorrow. This leads to the answer for Exercise #13-6: The two days of the week about which you should not worry are tomorrow and yesterday.

Are you spending too much time worrying and missing out on today? Can you concentrate and be in the here and now? Spending too much time worrying about losing, failing, or making mistakes will make you tense and anxious. Too much worrying predisposes you to stress, headaches, panic attacks, ulcers, and other related ailments. Most worry is self-inflicted and somewhat useless.

> *"Never cry over spilt milk, It could've been whiskey."*
>
> *- Pappy in Maverick*

Wasted Worries

* 40% of worries are about events which will never happen.
* 30% of worries are about events which already happened.
* 22% of worries are about trivial events.
* 4% of worries are about real events we cannot change.
* 4% of worries are about real events on which we can act.

The above chart indicates that 96 percent of the things we worry about are things we can't control. This signifies 96 percent of our worrying is wasted. In fact, it is even worse than that. Worrying about things we can control is wasted as well, since we can control these things. In other words, worrying about things we can't control is wasted because we can't control them, and worrying about things we can control is wasted because we can control these things. The result is 100 percent of our worrying is wasted. (Now you can worry about all the time you have been wasting while worrying.)

Spending time worrying about the past or future is a waste of energy. Creative people realize Murphy's law has some bearing on the way things will be; that is, "If anything can go wrong, it will."

Hurdles are a certainty in life. There is no way for the highly creative to eliminate all the hurdles. They realize many new hurdles will appear regularly, but they also realize there is a way to overcome virtually all hurdles.

Most, if not all, worrying about problems robs you of energy which can be channelled to solve these problems. Here is a good attitude for you to adopt: Ultimately nothing matters and so what if it did? If you can live this motto, most worries will be eliminated.

> *"It isn't the experience of today that drives men mad. It is the remorse for something that happened yesterday, and the dread of what tomorrow may disclose."*
>
> - Robert Jones Burdette

Giving Up Control To Be In Control

Many people say they want to be in total control at all times. They worry and are insecure when they feel out of control. The need for control can be self-defeating. The creatively alive people of this world say one important factor for being fully alive is having the ability to yield or give up the need to control. Of course, this goes against what we have allowed ourselves to believe.

If you have ever ridden a horse, you will have realized it is much easier to ride the horse in the direction it is going. Getting through life in this world is also easier if you ride with the world in the direction it's going. This means giving up the need to control the way everything is going to turn out. To illustrate the importance of giving up control in life, I find it useful to use this analogy:

> *Assume you are on a raft floating down a fast moving and highly treacherous river. The raft happens to capsize and you fall into the rapidly flowing water. There are two things you can do. One is to try and take control and fight the river. If you do this you are liable to end up injured, as a result of being thrown against the rocks. The second thing you can do is give up total control. The moment you give up control you will be in control. You are now going with the flow. The water doesn't go into the rocks. The water goes around the rocks.*

Life is a fast moving river. To get through life with a minimum of scrapes and bruises, we must learn how to go with the flow. Going with the flow means giving up control. It means surrendering to the notion that we don't know how anything is going to turn out.

The best way to be in control of our destinies is to give up control and not worry about how things are going to turn out. Too many factors beyond our control will destroy the best of plans.

Creatively alive people yield and go with the flow. In going with the flow, creatively alive people are acknowledging the importance of mastering the moment.

Don't Plan To Be Spontaneous

Unlike the majority of adults, creatively alive adults live the moment. Similarly, unlike the majority of adults, creatively alive adults can be spontaneous. I think Mark Twain was probably speaking of his lack of spontaneity as an adult when he said, "It usually takes me more than three weeks to prepare a good impromptu speech."

Creativity
Principle

**Be
Spontaneous**

Abraham Maslow, the famous humanist psychologist, believed spontaneity is a trait which is too often lost as people grow older. Maslow said, "Almost any child can compose a song or poem or a dance or a painting or a play or a game on the spur of the moment, without planning or previous intent." The majority of adults lose this ability, according to Maslow. Nevertheless, Maslow found a small fraction of adults did not lose this trait, and if they did, they regained it later in life. These are the self-actualized people who are achieving a state of outstanding mental health. Maslow called this a state of being fully human. He found self-actualized people to be spontaneous and highly creative while moving toward maturity.

Spontaneity is, for all intents and purposes, synonymous with creative living. Creatively alive people aren't inhibited; they can express their true feelings. They are able, like children, to play and act foolish. They also are able, on the spur of the moment, to decide to do something not in their plans for that day. Creative people also have no problem with impromptu speeches. They are more like children when they speak, rather than like adults.

How spontaneous are you? Do you always stick to your plans for the day? Do you always follow a set routine? How often do you ignore your plans and do something different? I have found when I do something spontaneous, unexpected and interesting things happen to me. Many times I wind up with rewarding experiences which I would have never achieved by sticking to my plans.

Watch children to refresh your notion of spontaneity. If you can be a child again, you can be spontaneous. Being spontaneous means challenging your plans; it means being able to try something new on the spur of the moment because it may be something you will enjoy. Although most accountants and engineers would probably try to plan to be more spontaneous, no one can plan spontaneity. "Planned spontaneity" is an oxymoron; spontaneous means unplanned.

"The only truly happy people are children and the creative minority."

- Jean Caldwell

Being spontaneous also means allowing more chance in your life. The more chance you let in your world, the more interesting your world will become. Let more people into your life. Communicate with them and express yourself to them, especially if they have a different viewpoint from your own. You might learn something new.

Remember to be spontaneous on a regular basis. Every day practice doing something which you haven't planned. On the spur of the moment, choose and do something new and exciting. It can be quite a small thing like taking a different route somewhere, eating in a different restaurant, or going to some new kind of entertainment. You can make your life much more interesting by introducing something novel in all your activities.

Happiness has to do with being engaged. This is true in the workplace. This is also true away from the workplace. Being engaged literally means being totally immersed in any task. It means doing just one thing at a time, and enjoying it for all it's worth. As they say in Zen, if you can't find it where you're standing, where do you expect to wander in search of it? The great minds of Eastern philosophy have always said, "Happiness is the way." What they have been saying is happiness is not a destination. It is nothing you look for; you create it. You don't have to go looking for happiness .... if that's where you're coming from.

14. Don't Put Off Your Procrastinating

Procrastinate And Be More Creative

One of the best ways for us to be more creative is to slow down and take our time in doing some tasks. We can actually be more productive by slowing down. Even procrastinating has its merits. By putting things off, we can be more efficient. This chapter is, in part, about the art of procrastination.

Attempt the following exercise to test your creativity.

Exercise #14-1   -   Twice As Fishy But Just As Square

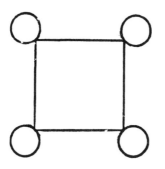

Ms. Colleen Waller, a wealthy businesswoman, had a lovely square fishpond on her Toronto estate. On each corner of the fishpond was a round lily pond, as shown above. Colleen wanted to double the size of her fishpond to accommodate twice as many fish; however, she didn't want to disturb her four lily ponds. Colleen wanted to keep the fish pond square. The lily ponds were required to be outside the perimeter of the fish pond.

She spoke to her gardener about this. He said it was impossible and all four lily ponds would have to be moved. How many lily ponds would you move?

Allow yourself 30 seconds to complete this problem.

What solution did you arrive at? Did you come to the conclusion that at least one lily pond didn't have to be moved? Optimally, no lily ponds have to be moved. There is a solution that makes this possible (see Appendix, page 186). Did you get this solution? If not, why not? You probably didn't get this better solution because I didn't allow you enough time. More time would have given you more opportunity to "see the light".

Not taking enough time with a problem is something most of us do too often. In doing so, we wind up with solutions which are at worst, totally unworkable, and at best, lacking in effectiveness. We must discipline ourselves to avoid rushing through situations when we can afford extra time for generating ideas. Sufficient time should be given for the generation of a large number of solutions. This necessitates delayed decision making.

"Your Honor, the jury members request the rest of the summer to think about it."

Delaying action on problems can be very important for generating highly creative solutions. Too often, we rush solving a problem when we would be better off to wait. Many problems and situations aren't as urgent as we make them out to be. When they aren't, it's best for us to take the time to let our minds play with the problem. Then our minds can report back at a later day.

Exercise #14-2 - Can You Remember Back When?

Assume that you have been given the task of planning a class reunion for all your classmates from grade 1 to grade 4. How many names can you think of in the next five minutes?

How many did you get? Ten to twenty? How many classmates did you have in those four years? Some of them moved. Some new ones joined your class over that period. You probably have missed naming a number of them. If you are given the rest of the day to think of all of them, you will undoubtedly get more names. Names will even come to you when you are thinking about something else. At the end of the day you may have thought of 60% of the classmates that you had.

Creativity Principle

Delay Your Decision

Then tomorrow you will think of more names if you are still focusing on this task. Of course, again some names will come to you while thinking about other things. Eventually, after two or three days, you will have remembered most of your former classmates.

Giving time for incubation of ideas works in much the same way as trying to think of your classmates' names over a long time period. Your subconscious mind is given a chance to generate more ideas than if you consciously try to come up with all available solutions in a short period of time. Sudden ideas generated in a limited time span tend to be the product of structured and rational thinking processes. Incubation over a long period of time overcomes the constraints of short term decision making.

> *"Ideas, like young wine, should be put in storage and taken up only after they have been given time to ferment and ripen."*
>
> *- Richard Strauss*

Try the following exercise allowing yourself two minutes.

Exercise #14-3   -   Breaking The Chain Of Demand

A wealthy businessman and his chauffeur are robbed on their way to the city by a group of modern-day bandits. Their limousine and nearly all of their possessions are stolen. All the businessman has left of any value is a gold chain with 23 links. The businessman is too old to walk long distances. He finds the nearest hotel and sends his chauffeur for money and a new car. The chauffeur will take 23 days to fetch a car and some money and return. The hotel owner demands that the businessman give him one gold link each day as security for future payment. The businessman does not want to give the hotel owner more links than the number of nights he has stayed at the hotel. He wants to recover his chain with the fewest possible links that have been cut. What must the businessman do to give the hotel owner one link a day but cut as few links as possible?

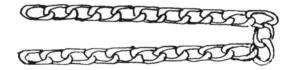

If you did what most people do with the above exercise, you determined that every second link had to be cut. This gives the minimum number cut as 11. Actually there is a better solution with a lower number of required cuts. If you take your time and approach this problem from other perspectives, you may see the optimum solution. Try it. We'll come back to this later.

Incubation involves putting the problem on the back burner. This allows us to attend to other matters while the problem simmers away in our sub-conscious. We get away from direct involvement with the problem. In this way we suspend judgment and allow ourselves the luxury of having the problem travel through our various states of mind. In time, we will have had several solutions come and go at unexpected times. Because these solutions will just pop out of nowhere, it is important that we write them down. Otherwise we stand the chance of forgetting some excellent solutions.

Allowing more time results in our experiencing greater perception. Associations with other stimulants generate new perspectives which we do not experience when we rush through the problem. We avoid the rigidity that we have in the initial stages. This results in new and more open observations which lead to interesting and sometimes stunning ideas.

> *"Learn to pause ... or nothing worthwhile will catch up to you."*
>
> *- Doug King, Poet*

In solving Exercise #14-3, you can just accept that 11 links have to be cut. However, if you decide to take more time, you likely will get a better solution. If you put this problem on the back burner of your mind, tomorrow or another day the solution can hit you out of nowhere. Suppose you are in a store paying for a $2.00 item with a $5.00 bill. The clerk gives you $3.00 (in $1 bills) back. An association of this transaction can be made to the problem of the businessman with the gold chain. Where may this lead?

At this point it may occur to you that this type of transaction can be made by the businessman and the hotel owner, only it will be with gold links and not dollars. (Hint: On a particular day, does the businessman have to deal with a denomination of only 1 gold link? Can't he give a higher denomination, say 3 links together, and get change, 2 single links, back? Where will this thinking lead to? Now play around with the problem for a better solution. The optimum solution to the problem is that only two links have to be cut. See if you can figure out which two links these are.

For most problems, various associations with unrelated items can be made during the incubation stage. This may lead to several good answers. A new problem may also arise. The problem may be that of choosing the best answer from the many outstanding ones you have generated. This is a good problem to have.

Generating More Stunning Solutions By Slowing Down

Disciplining yourself to avoid rushing through a problem is the first step in finding stunning or blockbuster solutions. This requires the presence of mind to convince yourself that the world is not going to come to an end if you do not make a decision today. Some problem solving is urgent; some is not. Once you have decided that you have the luxury of additional time, you are well on your way to finding a better answer. We see how taking time with Exercise #14-3 can lead to a much better solution (see Appendix, page 186 for the exact solution).

"A story must simmer in its own juice for months or even years before it's ready to serve."

- Edna Ferber

Looking for better solutions can be done consciously by stating the problem to yourself for several days. Reminding yourself of the problem can be done in many ways. Here are some of the ways to consciously attend to the problem in preparation for letting your subconscious mind do the work to find a blockbuster solution.

* Write your problem on several strips of paper. Leave these strips in various locations so that you come across them from time to time. Leave one in your briefcase, one in the medicine cabinet, one on the car dash, one on your office desk, and so on. In this way you will be reminded about your problem unexpectedly.

* Remind yourself of the problem while performing physical activities. Do this while walking, exercising, cleaning the house, or shovelling the walk. Whisper your problem while shaving or putting your make-up on.

* State your problem while meditating in private, daydreaming in your office, or resting on the sofa.

* State your problem to yourself the first thing in the morning after you get up. State it a second time and then leave it alone for a while.

It is important to note that you are not being asked to worry about your problem day and night. You are to consciously think about the problem at the various times with full confidence that an answer will appear in due time.

After several days of consciously thinking about your problem, the stunning answer may have appeared. If it has, the mission is complete. If it hasn't, then stop thinking about the problem consciously. Allow the problem to simmer in your sub-conscious for some time after. Seemingly, out of nowhere, answers will appear. Eventually, one will surface with a stunning effect. Eureka! Intuitively, you will know that this is the great one.

15. Be Persistent And Wind Up A Genius

Perseverance Helped Him Dance His Life Away

Throughout this book I have emphasized several principles of creativity and other tidbits of information for achieving satisfaction in life. The last principle of creativity not yet discussed in detail is just as important as any of the principles and tidbits already discussed.

Many years ago a young man mustered enough courage to ask a young lady to dance. After he had danced with her for a few minutes, the lady told him that he was a lousy dancer. She complained he danced like a truck driver.

For many people this experience would have been enough for them to decide to quit dancing for good. Watching television or sitting around bored would have appeared much better alternatives.

Nevertheless, this man developed a passion for dancing and continued to dance for many years after. He became known as one of the great dancers in modern times. At the time of his death in March of 1991, he had 500 dance schools named after him. He had at one time been on TV for 11 years straight, showing many different people, including truck drivers, how to dance.

> "You are never given a wish without also being given the power to make it true.
>
> You may have to work for it, however."
>
> - Richard Bach

By now you undoubtedly know I am talking about Arthur Murray. He became great at what he did because he was persistent. Aware of his own ability to learn and grow, he discovered his true potential.

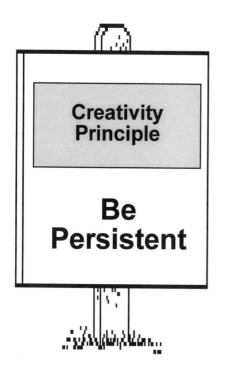

Creativity
Principle

Be
Persistent

Genius Is Nothing More Than Persistence Disguised

I can vouch for the power of persistence or perseverance since I have used them in my life. Today my books sell in the tens of thousands in USA and Canadian bookstores. I accept a few speaking engagements paying as much as $2000 plus expenses for a half hour. Sometimes I turn down certain lucrative speaking engagements because my leisure time is more important. Yet as recently as five years ago I would have gladly told you much of the information contained in my speeches and books for free. In fact, I would have treated you to an expensive dinner just so I could have someone to listen to me. (I was desperate to have someone on whom I could test my material.)

I recall several years ago sitting with a group of acquaintances in a restaurant discussing what it takes to be successful in life. When I stated my philosophy about creativity and what constitutes security in life, everyone else at the table told me I was either weird or crazy. When I was in the MBA program at the University of Alberta, I challenged the academics to change the outdated program and put creativity courses in it. Most MBA students and professors thought I was, if not a total basket case, then certainly on a different page than they were.

Despite the criticism I have taken over the last few years, I was able to follow my own philosophy and make it work to my advantage. One of the biggest reasons for my zest for living today is I enjoy what I am working at for a living. Since I don't have to work more than 4 or 5 hours a day, I also have a great balance between work and play. In fact, most of my work is play since I enjoy it so much. I wouldn't take a salary of $1,000,000 a year to work for anyone else, no matter what the job or title, simply because I enjoy my freedom.

The question is how did I get to where I am? I got here by being persistent. While the people with whom I graduated from the MBA program were making $75,000 a year, I was making $15,000 a year. I persevered even when I was living at the poverty level and was getting to the point where I wouldn't know where my next month's rent was coming from. I always felt if I stuck to what I enjoyed I could eventually make a living at it.

Now some people who a few years ago thought that my mental elevator didn't go to the top floor are willing to pay me for advice. Certain individuals from my graduating class think I am a marketing genius because I was able to make a self-published book a best-seller. I am no more a

> *"Persistence is what makes the impossible possible, the possible likely, and the likely definite."*
>
> *- Robert Half*

genius in marketing (or anything else for that matter) than other individuals with some knowledge of marketing and some common sense. What has helped me attain some of my important goals is my willingness to be persistent as well as my willingness to follow the other 16 principles of creativity mentioned in this book.

The power of persistence is remarkable. Here are two more examples of the power of persistence:

* Do you recognize any of these names? Captain Betts, Willie Delight, Jed Jackson, Buddy Links, Jimmy Malone, and Willy Williams. These were all stage names George Burns used early in his career as a vaudeville comedian. Burns admits his acts were so bad he frequently had to change his name to get booked again. However, his persistence paid off. Burns eventually developed an act people loved and he became a star.

* Thomas Edison is reported to have made several hundred experiments before he was successful in developing the light bulb. After about 500 attempts, Edison's assistant asked him "Why do you persist in this folly? You have tried 500 times and you have failed 500 times." Edison was quick to respond "Oh, but I have not failed even once. Now I know 500 ways of how not to make a light bulb." Of course, Edison's persistence eventually paid off with a workable light bulb.

You can do the same with your life. Persist in your plans and endeavors and you may wind up a genius (or a star) in the eyes of others less persistent than you. At that point you will know that genius is nothing more than persistence or perseverance disguised.

Don't Be A Victim Of Incorrect Thinking

The Globe and Mail's editorial recently talked about how the 1990s constitute the decade of the victim. Rather than take responsibility for their lives, many people today are taking the easy way out by trying to establish themselves as victims of society, the economy, a conspiracy, or some alleged discrimination.

Victims tend to be people driven by negative motivation. Affected by their own insecurities and past failures, people with negative motivation in life just go through the motions. They complain all the time, they start things and don't finish them, they make the same mistakes again and again, and nothing around them seems to work. The saddest thing is they aren't aware of how negative they are.

Negative people have a desire for comfort and a desire to avoid failure. This usually results in low intention, or complete inaction. Although fear can be a positive motivator, it more often than not negatively motivates us to react in ways that contribute little or nothing to our satisfaction. Fear, for the most part, induces us to react negatively, rather than positively.

Other unhealthy modes of thinking such as the one-big-deal syndrome act as negative motivation. The one-big-deal syndrome is one of those adolescent-rescue fantasies we all had in our younger years. Unfortunately, I know many people who have carried these adolescent-rescue fantasies well into their 50s and 60s. Adolescent fantasies are favorites of adults with low self-esteem and intention.

These are some variations of the one-big-deal syndrome: If I could only win a $5-million lottery, then I would be happy; if I could only get a new relationship with someone exciting, then I wouldn't be so bored; and if I could get an exciting, high paying job, then I could start living. People afflicted with the one-big-deal syndrome are looking for an easy way to happiness, when none exists. Waiting for the one big deal avoids the effort required to make life work.

There are many other thinking patterns which can signal an inadequate intention in life as well as low self-esteem. If you have any of the following beliefs or thoughts, you are subjecting yourself to negative motivators that won't contribute anything to your success.

166

- I have problems in life that are unique. Nobody else could possibly have these whoppers.
- You can't tell me anything that I don't already know.
- When someone dislikes me, I feel bad about myself.
- I should not be subject to the discomfort of failure.
- The world ought to be fair, especially to me.
- People are so different from the way they should be.
- Changing myself is impossible because I was born this way.
- My less-than-perfect parents are to blame for the way I am.
- Governments don't do enough for common people like myself.
- Governments should do more to protect our jobs in the health, teaching, ..., etc. fields.
- The Government doesn't do enough for our industry.
- I am at a disadvantage because I am a woman, a member of a minority, a white male, ..., etc.
- I am disadvantaged because I do not have enough money, am not beautiful, and don't know the right people.
- Why isn't everyone as nice to me as I am to everyone else?
- I don't have a high enough education to accomplish anything.

> *"Success is counted the sweetest by those who never succeed."*
> - Emily Dickinson

If you regularly have any of the above thoughts, you are setting yourself up for much grief and pain. You are consciously or subconsciously generating excuses for not taking the steps you must take to make your life work. You are also a victim of incorrect thinking. Whose? Your own! Whose else?

> *"Argue for your limitations and sure enough they are yours."*
> - Richard Bach

Blaming the world for being a lousy place is a good way to guarantee that the world will continue to remain lousy for you. Even when you think you see the light at the end of the tunnel, it will be an oncoming train. You will end up giving credence to an old Norwegian adage: "Nothing is so bad it can't get worse".

Excuses are valid if you are severely handicapped or if you live in a third-world country with virtually no opportunity. The United States and Canada still offer incredible opportunity for capable individuals. For the second time in three years Canada was chosen by the United Nations as the best place to live in the world in 1992 in terms of human development; the United States was chosen eighth overall. The ranking was based on average income, life expectancy, and educational attainment.

> *"Liberty means responsibility. That's why most men dread it."*
>
> *- George Bernard Shaw*

Despite Canada's ranking as the best place in the world to live, I find many people don't see the opportunity which exists in the country. Many Canadians spend most of their time complaining about how bad things are and how rough life is. And most of these people I am talking about aren't severely disadvantaged. I am talking about healthy, able, well-educated, and previously or presently highly paid individuals who are spoiled and suffer from the-world-owes-me-a-living syndrome.

I point to what Douglas Cardinal, probably Canada's most renowned architect, recently said. Cardinal, of native Indian heritage, believes Canadians have something to learn from his philosophy:

> *"Canada doesn't have an economic problem but an attitude problem. We're splashing around feeling sorry for ourselves because our economy is down. What a bunch of nonsense. That's an attitude. We've got an attitude problem. The doom and gloom doesn't affect me because I refuse to participate .... We can create anything we wish. It's our own attitude that puts us in the situation we're in. Those laid off from jobs can see their predicaments as setbacks or challenges."*

> *"The thorns which I have reaped are of the tree I planted."*
>
> *- Lord Byron"*

I find that Americans in general have a better attitude than Canadians. Even though the USA was chosen eighth overall to Canada's first place standing in the 1992 United Nations poll, Americans seem to appreciate their country and the opportunity it offers much more than Canadians appreciate their country.

Whether you are a Canadian or an American, I must warn you of the dangers of the victim mentality. You will never be liberated if this is your game in life. How can you? You will always set it up so that you are a victim to satisfy your perverted belief system.

If you are a truly liberated person, you know there is discrimination of all sorts out there as well as many other roadblocks; however, you will decide to go for it anyway. Liberation takes effort and persistence - not someone else's but your own.

Walking The Talk Rather Than Talking The Walk

Having learned the principles of creativity won't guarantee that you will gain more success and satisfaction from life, just as owning a horse won't guarantee you will ride the horse and appreciate it. You have to motivate yourself in some way to do what is necessary to attain satisfaction at anything worth doing. You must also forget the excuses.

Exercise #15-1 - A Common Non-Excuse

What did these people all have in common?

* Thomas Edison (Inventor)
* Sophia Loren (Actor)
* Al Pacino (Actor)
* Bobby Fisher (Former world chess champion)
* Peter Jennings (TV Newscaster on ABC)
* Soichiro Honda (founder of Honda Motor Corp.)
* Buckminister Fuller (Inventor of Geodesic Dome)

> *"Success is just a matter of luck. Ask any failure."*
>
> *- Karl Wilson*

Many people use the excuse of their limited education for not pursuing more creative and satisfying careers. Well guess what? All of the above people were all either elementary or high school dropouts. Thomas Edison had only three weeks formal education. Another handicap was deafness from which he suffered for most of his life. Did these two stop him? No! His inventions dramatically changed our lives.

So let's forget the excuses. Just because something is difficult is no reason for not doing it. I encounter many people who dream of writing a book, but never get around to it due to excuses. I should point out I failed my first-year university English course three times before I finally passed it; nonetheless, I am still able to write books.

It is one thing to acknowledge problems in life and decide what must be done to change. Most people can reach this point. Where most people fail is in doing something about it. Inaction renders the knowledge of the problem and what to do about it worthless. There is an old saying "talk is cheap because supply exceeds demand". Many people talk about the wonderful things they are going to do in life, but never get around to doing very many of them. Talking about the walk is one thing; walking the talk is another issue in itself.

The difference between high achievers and low achievers is high achievers think actively and not passively. Studies on high achievers indicate they can take a lot of time to just think about things. Their accomplishment is not based only on being active physically, but also on their ability to meditate, ponder, and daydream.

Achievers think about being doers and attaining a sense of accomplishment. Eventually they do what they have been planning to do; this makes the difference in their lives. They know making a difference, whether in leisure pursuits or in business affairs, means having to light the fire rather than just waiting around to be warmed by someone else's fire.

> *"There is nothing brilliant nor outstanding in my record, except perhaps this one thing: I do the things that I believe ought to be done .... And when I make up my mind to do a thing, I act."*
>
> *- Theodore Roosevelt*

Walking the talk is about commitment. Many people use the word commitment but they don't really know what it means. Using the word, because it sounds nice, does not represent commitment. The majority say they are committed to being happy and successful in life. Their actions represent the opposite of commitment. When they learn their goal requires time, energy, and sacrifice, they give up the goal.

Here is a simple test to determine how committed you are to your goals and making your life work: Do you do the things you say you are going to do? This applies to seemingly insignificant items like calling a person when you say you will. If you are not doing the small things that you say you will, I have a hard time believing you will be committed to larger goals. If commitment is lacking in your life, you won't attain very much satisfaction in the long run.

Your actions are the only thing that will attest to your commitment. A seriousness about commitment will mean you have the intense desire to achieve your goals, no matter what barrier or wall appears in your way. "As you sow, so shall you reap." In other words, whatever you put in the universe will be reflected back to you. It takes action - plenty of it - to get fulfillment and satisfaction in your life. Don't be like most people who don't follow through with action. Your positive attitude and enthusiasm for living are the ingredients for being committed to action, and a life that works. When it comes to commitment, always remember these words of wisdom from the Buddhists: "To know and not to do is not yet to know."

16. Creativity Is A Three-Letter Word

The Only Thing Certain Is Uncertainty

In the preceding chapters, we looked at principles which I consider vital for our creative success. These are principles that, if followed regularly, can make a big difference in our lives. Even by using these principles infrequently, we have a chance to impact substantially upon our lives and those of others.

The question is "Is our success in our careers assured if we follow all the creativity principles?" Before I answer that, first let us look at the world as it looks today. Following are the conditions that reflect the modern world. This is the climate that everyone has to deal with; we have virtually no choice about whether or not we can escape these conditions.

* Intense and accelerating change
* Unpredictable events
* Unstable and chaotic conditions
* Impact of high technology
* Downsizing and cutbacks
* Powerful consumer forces
* Global economy

> "The only modern fairy tale is the one that begins: Once upon a time, there was a secure job."
>
> - Unknown Wise Person

Welcome to the exciting 1990s. These conditions signify that no individual can take anything for granted in the workplace. We are seeing that change is not only rapid but accelerating at a torrid pace. People felt the 1980s were a time of rapid change. The rate of change of the 1980s now looks like a snail's pace (and a piece of cake) in comparison to the rate of change in the 1990s.

> *"The more unpredictable the world becomes, the more we rely on predictions."*
>
> *- Steve Rivkin*

As we approach the mid-point of the 1990s, we can expect the rate of change to increase at a greater rate than the early 1980s The rate of change we are dealing with today may look like a snail's pace towards the end of this decade. What this means is there is but one certainty in today's world. If you still haven't noticed, in the 1990s the only certainty is uncertainty.

Just look at today's headlines in national publications such as the *Globe & Mail*, *USA Today*, and *Fortune*. You will read: "Shrinking Possibilities For Architects"; "The Pain Of Downsizing"; "Why So Many Managers Are Quitting Corporate America To Strike Out On Their Own; "What's Happening To Jobs In America"; and "How The New Executive Unemployed Are Coping". Looking at these headlines confirms uncertainty is the one thing we can count on in the workplace; beyond this there are no guarantees.

So the warning is even if we follow all the creativity principles in this book, our success isn't certain. Then why should we follow and apply these principles and techniques? Simply because our chances for creative success are increased by at least 10,000 fold when we persist in following these principles. Increasing our odds by this much makes it all worthwhile. Being persistent in being creative will have its payoffs on most, if not all, projects we undertake.

The importance of being creative in today's world cannot be overemphasized. Paul Torrence, an expert in creativity, states:

> *"The genius of the future will be the creative mind adapting itself to the shape of things to come......The skills of creative thinking must be recognized as mankind's most important adaptability skills. Such skills must become basic to the curriculum of schools, homes, business, and other agencies."*

To deal effectively with today's world changing at an unprecedented pace, your opinions, beliefs, and values shouldn't be carved in stone. Avoid being a rigid person and your life will be a lot easier in the new world.

Some people think changing values, beliefs, or opinions represents weakness. On the contrary, the ability to change represents strength by those willing to change and grow in life.

There is much to be said for the saying that only the foolish and dead never change their beliefs and opinions. As I implied before, no matter who you are, you can change. I want to stress that the more inflexible and less perceptual you are, the more problems you will have in living and adjusting to our rapidly changing world.

> *"Faced with having to change our views or prove that there is no need to do so, most of us immediately get busy on the proof."*
>
> *- John Kenneth Galbraith*

As stated in the preface, my experience in teaching creativity seminars reveals that people who most need to change their thinking are most resistant to change. The opposite is true with highly adaptive and creative people. To them, change is exciting. They are always willing to challenge their points of view, and they are willing to change them when necessary.

Never challenging our points of view to see if they are still valid has at least two inherent dangers:

- The first danger is we may get locked into one way of thinking, without seeing other alternatives which may be more appropriate.
- The second danger is we may adopt a set of values which at the time makes a lot of sense. Time will pass; with time, things will change. The original values will no longer be appropriate because of the changes, but we will still continue to function with the original, outmoded values.

The 1990s and beyond will be frustrating and unrewarding for those who choose not to use their creative abilities. For those who develop their creative skills and persist in using them, the times will offer many opportunities. The future belongs to those who will learn how to cope with and thrive on uncertainty. People who have learned to think laterally, search for many solutions, look for the obvious, take risks, celebrate failure, fully explore all ideas, and like chaos will be at the forefront of business. They will be the people making a difference as entrepreneurs in their own businesses or as leaders of the progressive organizations of the new world.

> *"It's what you learn after you know it all that counts."*
>
> *- John Wooden*

A New Paradigm For Success

Some people will think this book is a how-to book on how to become rich and famous. Creative success doesn't mean being rich and famous. If you aren't receiving satisfaction from your life and you think that fame and fortune are what will get you there, you will require nothing short of a paradigm shift to get you on the right track. A paradigm is a belief or explanation of some situation that a group of people share. A shift from an old paradigm to a new paradigm is a distinctive, new way of thinking about old problems.

> *"I don't want to be the richest man in the graveyard."*
>
> *- Song by Ben Kerr, Toronto Busker at Yonge and Bloor*

Your paradigm shift should involve a change of your beliefs about success. Success is possible without being rich or famous. Success peddled by society means a high-paying job, celebrity status, a big home, and a luxury car. This isn't the only way to define success; success can be defined in many ways. With a paradigm shift, success takes on a different meaning.

Truly creative, successful people show a concern for the world around them. Their focus is not just on themselves and their career or business but also on the environment, the poor, the disadvantaged, and the need for world peace.

Today being an entrepreneur has become a goal for many. If you want to be an entrepreneur because it will bring you fame and fortune, you ain't no genuine entrepreneur. As a true entrepreneur you should be looking at how you are making the world a better place to live for others. The satisfaction you will receive from making a modest living selling a product which enhances the lives of other people is ten fold over the satisfaction you will receive if you make lots of money from something not that beneficial to the world such as being involved in a pyramid scheme or selling contraband cigarettes.

Vince Lombardi's "winning is the only thing" also shouldn't be construed as success. Some people consider The Buffalo Bills "losers" because they lost the Superbowl four years in a row. How many other NFL football teams have appeared in the Superbowl four years in a row? This team is one of the most successful ever and many bubbleheads are calling its players "losers".

I like Ralph Waldo Emerson's definition of success.

What Is Success?

* To laugh often and love much;
* To win the respect of intelligent persons and the affection of children;
* To earn the approval of honest critics and endure the betrayal of false friends;
* To appreciate beauty;
* To find the best in others;
* To give of one's self without the slightest thought of return;
* To have accomplished a task, whether by a healthy child, a rescued soul, a garden patch or a redeemed social condition;
* To have played and laughed with enthusiasm and sung with exaltation;
* To know that even one life has breathed easier because you have lived;
* This is to have succeeded.

- Ralph Waldo Emerson

It is always hard to resist thinking of a successful person as someone who is rich and famous. Notice that all of what constitutes Emerson's definition of success is possible without fame and fortune. Fame and fortune are okay as a bonus in life but they aren't essential for having lived creatively and productively.

The obsession with fame and fortune indicates shortcomings in the values common to North American society. If you have adopted these values, you may want to consider seeing things differently. Having strict beliefs that fame and fortune are necessary for happiness and success will leave you dissatisfied and unfulfilled.

Being a creative thinker allows you to see that modifying your values for a more modest emphasis on fame and materialism has its merits. Someone who owns many gadgets, trinkets, and other "stuff" is not a better person than the individual who has less. The addiction to stuff tends to alienate us from other people and the environment.

> *"If you want to hear about the power and glory of wealth, ask a man who's seeking it. But if you want to learn of wealth's burden's and difficulties, ask a man who's been wealthy a long time."*
>
> *- Stanley Goldstein*

In the higher order in life, stuff around us - cars, houses, stereos, jobs - they're facilities and nothing else. They are not the source of our happiness. The things we own, the places we live, and the jobs we have are secondary in importance. True success shouldn't be measured by what we own or what we do for a living. Our real essence is of a higher order. The only things that should matter in the end are how well did we live: what did we learn, how much did we laugh and play, and how much did we love. This is the real stuff of life!

In regards to fame and fortune, here's something to think about: No matter how rich and popular you become in your life, the number of people at your funeral will depend upon the weather.

Success At Not Working Is Important Too

If you want to enhance the quality of your life, challenging your thinking about work and leisure is another good area on which to focus. Working long hours is supposed to be the key to success. Contrary to public belief, this is seldom the case. For some mysterious reason, people, who espouse the virtues of hard work in our society, overlook the fact that several million people keep their noses to the grindstone throughout their careers, and wind up with nothing but flat noses. They certainly don't fulfill their dreams.

> *"If hard work was such a wonderful thing, the rich would have kept it all to themselves."*
>
> *- Lane Kirkland*

Your ability to enjoy leisure will be determined by how much you have been able to avoid being brainwashed by society. Don't work because it's moral to do so. Working at an unpleasant job when it is necessary for one's survival is rational. Working at an unpleasant job, when one is financially well-off and doesn't have to work, is irrational. Nevertheless, many well-off people toil away at unpleasant jobs, because they believe it is moral to be working.

Most people haven't stopped to consider that a great deal of harm may result from the belief that work is a virtue. Although it is necessary for our survival, working long hours doesn't contribute as much to individual well-being as many think it does.

Just to set things straight, I am not saying that we should avoid as much work as possible. You may have erroneously assumed I suffer from the fear of work (which is called ergophobia by psychologists). On the contrary, I still get a great deal of satisfaction from most work I choose to do. Writing and publishing this book is one example.

"Give it heck guys. Work hard! That's how I got my start."

My point is that working for the sake of working can be detrimental to our well-being and enjoyment in life. This is by no means a new revelation. Bertrand Russell, a little while ago, stated that North America's attitude toward work and leisure was outdated, and contributed to the misery in society. In his essay, *In Praise Of Idleness*, Russell stated:

"The morality of work is the morality of slaves, and the modern world has no need of slavery."

I would like to have you believe that Bertrand borrowed this line from me, but this would sound far fetched, considering he wrote this in 1932, over 60 years ago. Reading Russell's essay now is eye opening due to its relevance today. It is interesting to see how little our values have changed in 60 years, although our world has dramatically changed. Old values and beliefs are hard to surrender.

If you look at creative people, you will see they have success at work and play. Here are the traits of the highly creative who have a good balance in their lives.

- **Creative people are different.** Most people spend their time trying to fit in with the rest of society. They conform because they are approval seekers and don't want to stand out. Creative people have no problem being different. They stand out. Whether at work or at play, they don't care what others think. They do not let society dictate how they should behave. They won't engage in small talk because it is the proper and polite thing to do. To the creative, conformity is dull and interferes with one's ability to do the new and rewarding. Because

177

creative people aren't approval seekers, they have more freedom to pursue leisure activities which contribute to personal growth and satisfaction.

- **Creative people are comfortable with change and uncertainty.** In today's chaotic world creative people whether at work or at play welcome change and aren't threatened by uncertainty. With change comes an opportunity to learn and grow. People who know how to use their creative abilities are the ones who are not only coping with, but thriving on the chaos in the modern world.

- **Creative people are enthusiastic about life.** Enthusiasm is different from excitement. Where excitement is an occasional outburst of energy or joy, enthusiasm is an internal energy that flows from one's essence. Creative people have taken the time to develop an essence and a rich internal world. They project a constant zest for living, and don't have to rely on outside influences to excite them. Although unenthusiastic people display occasional excitement from external stimulants, they have little zest for life. Creative people are capable of enjoying television, parties, night clubs, taverns, and the like, but you won't find them spending too much time with these. Instead, you will find them enjoying more rewarding activities, ones which unenthusiastic people miss out on.

> *"You only live once. But if you work it right, once is enough."*
>
> *- Fred Allen*

- **Creative people are self-motivated with defined goals.** They set goals which they work towards. Goals give them a purpose. To achieve these goals requires motivation. Because creative people are doers, they don't have to go and hear motivational speakers like unmotivated people do. They are self-directed enough to just go out and do it. When creative people lose jobs, and along with it their purpose, they create another purpose. The new purpose is as important or more important than the one they had in a career or a job.

- **Creative people can enjoy themselves when alone.** These individuals don't always have to be with people. They relish being alone regularly. Their motto is, "It is better to be alone than in bad company". Because they aren't overly dependent on people, they develop a few, quality friendships rather than a lot of superficial ones. To them, aloneness is not synonymous with loneliness. They know that people who always have to be with others are some of the loneliest people around. Creative people not only enjoy being alone, they often demand their privacy. They have a rich inner world to compliment their rich outer world. Their ability to be alone makes it easy for them to have a satisfying time when other people are just not available to be with them. Yet you will find creative people to be some of the most sociable people around.

> *"My husband said he needed more space, so I locked him outside."*
>
> *- Roseanne Barr*

- **Creative people experience freedom from failure.** They know how to fail; they do not view failure in the same way as the majority. Failure, to creative people, is a means to success. They realize that the best way to double their success rate is to double their failure rate. To be successful in one's career, a person must have had many setbacks. There is no difference in achieving success in one's life of leisure. Only by having experienced regular failure will one have achieved a great deal of success.

- **Creative people are adventurous.** They like to explore the world around them. They like to travel to new destinations, to meet new people, and to see new things. Being moderate risk takers, they will try activities with an element of danger. Naturally curious, creative people want to learn every present moment of their lives. There are unlimited opportunities for doing, thinking, feeling, loving, laughing, and living.

It is obvious from the above traits displayed by creative people that your attitude towards work and play is the most important trait you can possess. By shaping your own attitude, you make life what it is. No one but you gets to make your own bed. No one but you can ever put in the effort to make your life work. No one but you can generate the joy, the enthusiasm, or the motivation to live your life to the fullest.

I can't overstate the importance of experiencing the joy of not working. If you still aren't convinced how precious leisure time is, here is something you should consider: How many people have you heard about who on their death bed said, "I wish I would have worked more"? There probably weren't many.

Thinking For A Change

You should have noticed by now that creative living is more than just having a "great idea". Now you must do something with what you have learned. Activity and inner mobility will go a long way. You have to love the world to be of service to it. Always try to seek growth, not perfection. You are the creator of the context in which you view things. It is up to you to find a way to enjoy the activities you undertake. Let your interests be as wide as possible; the variety in life makes the effort to experience that variety well worthwhile.

"Oh, to reach the point of death, and realize one has not lived at all"

-Thoreau

Looking past your present beliefs and perceptions may open up many new dimensions to living. Develop a presence of mind to question everything you believe. Learn to weed out old, unworkable beliefs. At the same time, develop the ability to adopt new values and fresh behaviors to see whether they are workable. By challenging and changing your thinking, you set the stage for fresh perspectives and new values to replace outmoded beliefs.

We can change the quality of our lives by changing the context in which we view our circumstances. Two people can be faced with the same situation, such as being fired from a job. Yet one will view it as a blessing, and the other will view it as a curse. Changing the context of the situation depends on our ability to challenge and be flexible in our thinking. Most of us do not take the time to reflect upon what we are thinking, and why. To produce change in our thinking, we must start thinking for a change.

By challenging and changing your thinking, you set the stage for fresh perspectives and new values to replace outmoded beliefs. The question you should ask yourself is "Do I want to 'think for a change' and make a creative difference in my life and the lives of others?"

Once you have decided you want to make a difference in this world, you must be committed to making that difference. Don't be a carbon copy; instead be an original. Take the time to think about how you are limiting yourself in your life by trying to be like everyone else. If you have an unhealthy need to always fit in and be accepted by everyone, you are setting yourself up for a life of boredom. In addition, chances are others will find you rather boring. In other words, if you want your life to be boring, then conform and be dull; if you want your life to be interesting and exciting, then be different.

You are the only person who can choose for you to be creative. You are the only person who can do the work that needs to be done. You are the only person who can supply the energy, the enthusiasm, the courage, the unreasonableness, the spontaneity, the discipline, and the persistence that is required. Your career and personal life will be as adventurous, exciting, and rewarding as you want them to be.

> *"Here is a test to find whether your mission on earth is finished:*
>
> *If you're alive, it isn't."*
>
> *- From Illusions by Richard Bach*

Today's world is filled with an infinite number of possibilities for using the principles from this book. You must remember to refrain from being a know-it-all. In experiencing the joy of not knowing it all, you must also remember this: Creativity is not society. Creativity is not your organization. Creativity is not your education. Creativity is not your intelligence. And Creativity is not your knowledge. Just what is creativity? Creativity is your natural ability to think in new and wonderful ways and make a big difference in this world.

Creativity is a three-letter word. Creativity is _____!

(For the one and only right answer to this, see Appendix, page 186.)

If you have enjoyed this book and have any thoughts, comments, or experiences that you would like to let me know about, I would be happy to hear from you. Address all letters to:

Ernie Zelinski
P.O. Box 4072
Edmonton, Alberta
Canada, T6E 4S8

Appendix

Solutions To Exercises

Exercise #1-1 - How to make an egg stand on its end

* Use some glue.
* Use some gum.
* Put some salt on the table.
* Use an egg holder.
* Use a nail.
* Gently tap an unboiled egg until the shell is slightly broken and you will have no trouble standing it on its end.
* Wait until the equinox and stand the egg on its end using the electromagnetic forces.
* With a pen write "end" on the side of the egg, then lay the egg on its side where end is written and you have the egg standing on its "end".

Exercise #1-3 - What do a book, bed, and beer have in common?

* All are represented by words which spelled backwards make no sense.
* All of them put you to sleep.
* All can be found in most hotel rooms.
* If dropped from a high rise apartment, all can be damaged.
* Fish don't normally need any of them.
* All can be bought in a shopping mall.
* You don't have to be an intellectual to enjoy any of them.
* All have been stolen.
* All can be imagined.
* You can't take any of them with you when you die.
* All have been given as gifts.
* All can be enjoyed alone.
* All can be used to enhance sex (if you are creative).
* All have been used in making movies.
* David Letterman has talked about all three on his show.
* All can be purchased for under $1000.
* All have been used in one way or another to make money.
* All have got people in trouble. (ie. book - Satanic Verses)
* All are not standard equipment on a Rolls Royce.
* All have a lot in common with a boot.
* They all don't have a lot in common with seagulls.
* When frozen, all three are solids.

Exercise #2-3

Add the line as shown above and turn the page upside down to get VI.

Exercise #2-4   Part A

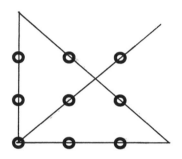

Exercise #2-4   Part B

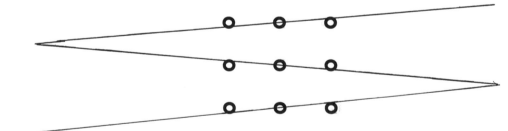

Exercise #2-4   Part C

This part has at least seven different solutions. One is to cut out the nine circles with a pair of scissors and line them up. Then draw a straight line through them. Another solution is to use a very wide line.

Exercise #6-3 - The Advantages Of Drinking On The Job

Plus	**Minus**	**Interesting**
• People will be more creative	• Safety goes down	• What would happen if we allowed drinking on special occassions?
• Employees want to come to work	• More people falling asleep	• How many people would actually drink on the job?
• Better communication	• Productivity goes down	
• Great way to find out who the alcoholics are	• Need more washrooms	
• Good way to make extra revenue for the company	• More Affairs (This could be a plus as well)	
	• Could lead to fights	

Exercise #8-7

The truck owner had taken some paint and modified the Grafitti to read:

FORD

Exercise #8-9

The man is Chinese because his mother and father were.

Chapter 9 - Mind Bender #2

The Prime Minister bought the numbers 2 and 4 for the address on his house.

Chapter 9 - Rebus Exercises

Ha! I bet you thought this was going be easy. To make it a little more difficult I have mixed up the solutions.

bad spell of the flu	split decision	miscalculation
scatter brain	about turn	equal rights
Times Square	mixed signals	whitewash
drawing on my knowledge	salary gap	reverse logic
inequality of the sexes	triple play	I am under the gun
paradigm shift	U-turn	toy box
time out	divided factions	long weekend
missing man	they are after me	unfinished business
I see you are creative	shattered dreams	elevator going up
inclined to be honest	see-through blouse	parachutes
part-time	black eye	freeways
being on time	afternoon tea	way up

Exercise #12-3

1. This was supposed to stand for "four pair equals eight". However a former girlfriend of mine gave her second answer to this as "foreplay is essential".

2. J. stands for Jaguar

3. F. stands for foot

4. E. stands for east

5. N. stands for north

6. A. stands for America

7. C. stands for century

8. Z. stands for zero

9. S. stands for San

10. R. stands for Ronald

11. Y. stands for your

12. S. stands for saved

13. U. stands for up

14. Y. stands for year

15. R. stands for rolling

16. W. stands for wife

17. D stands for day

18. S. stands for saw

19. D. stands for day

20. P. stands for Post

21. P. stands for Paul

22. Y. stands for year

23. M. stands for Madonna

24. N. stands for New

25. M. stands for months

Exercise #13-1

1. Pay Attention, 2. Pay Attention, 3. Pay Attention

Exercise #14-1

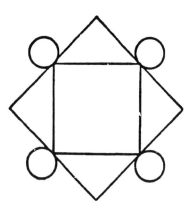

Exercise #14-3

Only two links need be cut. If the businessman cuts only the 7th and 11th links, he will have 2 single links, and one chain each of 3 links, 6 links, and 12 links. With these it is possible for the businessman to increase his payment of one link a day for 23 days. For example, on the fifth day he will give the 2 single links and the chain of 3 links.

Chapter 16 - Page 181

Bibliography And Recommended Books On Creativity

Tony Buzan's and Barry Buzan's *The Mind Map Book* (BBC Books, 1993)

Ira Flatow's *They All Laughed* (HarperPerennial, 1993)

Robert L. Shock's *Why Didn't I Think Of That?* (New American Library Books, 1982)

Michael Ray's and Rochelle Myers' *Creativity In Business* (Doubleday & Co., 1986)

William C. Miller's *The Creative Edge* (Addison-Wesley, 1986)

Robert J. Kriegel's *If it ain't broke, BREAK IT!* (Warner Books, 1991)

Charles Tompson's *What A Great Idea!* (HarperPerennial, 1992)

Charles Tompson's *"Yes, But....." The Top 40 Killer Phrases And How To Fight Them* (HarperBusiness, 1993)

Roger von Oech's *A Whack On The Side Of The Head* (Warner Books, 1983)

Roger von Oech's *A Kick In The Seat Of The Pants* (Harper & Row, 1986)

Edward DeBono's *Lateral Thinking* (Penguin Books, 1973)

Edward DeBono's *Six Thinking Hats* (Key Porter Books, 1985)

Paul Torrance's *The Search For Satori & Creativity* (Creative Education Foundation & Creative Synergetic Associates, 1979)

Eugene Raudsepp's *Growth Games For The Creative Manager* (Perigee Books, 1987)

Vincent Nolan's *Problem Solving* (Sphere Books, 1987)

Kurt Hanks' and Jay Parry's *Wake Up Your Creative Genius* (Crisp Publications, 1991)

Bibliography And Recommended Books On Creativity

(Continued)

Don Koberg's and Jim Bagall's *The Universal Traveler* (Crisp Publications, 1991)

Denis E. Waitley's *Winning The Innovation Game* (Berkley, 1989)

Michael LeBoeuf's *Imagineering - How To Profit From Your Creative Powers* (Berkley, 1986)

Arthur B. VanGundy's *Training Your Creative Mind* (Prentice-Hall, 1982)

Gerald I. Nierenberg's *The Art Of Creative Thinking* (Simon & Schuster, 1982)

Barbara Sher's *Wishcraft - How To Get What You Really Want* (Ballantine Books, 1979)

Faith Popcorn's *The Popcorn Report* (Doubleday, 1991)

Richard Bach's *Illusions: The Adventures Of A Reluctant Messiah* (Dell, 1977)

Peter Hanson's *The Joy Of Stress* (Hanson Stress Management Org., 1985)

Shakti Gwain's *Living In The Light* (Whatever Publishing, 1986)

John Naisbitt's and Patricia Aburdene's *Megatrends 2000* (William Morrow & Co., 1990)

Antoine de Saint Exupery's *The Little Prince* (Harcourt, Brace, Jovanocich, Inc., 1943)

About The Author

Ernie Zelinski is the author of the recent best-seller *The Joy Of Not Working*, a book which has inspired thousands of individuals in Canada and the United States to create a better life-style for the 1990s. He is also a professional speaker on creativity applied to work and play.

Ernie has an Engineering degree and a Master's in Business Administration. As a part-time instructor in business, he has taught his principles of creativity to students at the University of Alberta in Edmonton and Simon Fraser University and City University in Vancouver.

Ernie lives in Edmonton and spends as much time as he can in Vancouver, which he considers his second home. He has been 35 years old for the last several years, because he likes the age 35. Cycling and tennis are his two favorite sports. Although he doesn't own a motorcycle, Ernie is a member of the Lemmings Motorcycle Club. He watches television about once a week. He reads every day and prefers non-fiction over fiction.

Because he is a connoisseur of leisure, Ernie tries to maintain a four-hour work day and work only four days a week. He has leisurely started writing his third "The Joy Of NOT" book which he plans to complete some time in the near or distant future. Ernie is single, has never been married, and is patiently waiting for his soulmate to make her appearance.

Speeches & Seminars By Ernie Zelinski

Let Ernie Zelinski custom design a seminar or keynote speech for your next convention, meeting, management retreat, or company sponsored cruise. He is a master at applying creativity to both business and leisure. To hear Ernie is to learn how to be more creative and innovative on the job, and how to strike a balance between work and play.

As a professional speaker, he has spoken to audiences at many conferences and management retreats hosted by organizations such as BC Hydro, Canadian Association of Pre-Retirement Planners, Canadian Association of Insurance Women, Certified General Accountants of BC, and Transport Canada. These are his popular topics:

* **"Thinking Way Out In Left Field"**

    How individuals can be more creative in the workplace.

* **"The Joy Of Not Working"**

    How individuals can enhance their lives with quality leisure.

* **"Profiting From Creativity At Work Or Play"**

    How people can create more satisfying life-styles at work and play.

You can book Ernie Zelinski for a speech or seminar by writing or calling:

Pauline Price or Linda Davidson
Can*Speak Presentations
North Vancouver, BC, V7L 1V3
Phone (604) 986-6887
Toll Free Number (In Canada)
Phone (800) 665-7376

Ernie Zelinski
Visions International Publishing
P.O. Box 4072
Edmonton, Alberta
Canada, T6E 4S8
Phone (403) 436-1798

The Joy Of Not Knowing It All

A Book For The Creative And Uncreative

Whether you are an artist, poet, or businessperson, this entertaining resource is designed to help you profit from creativity at work and play. In a highly competitive and rapidly changing world *The Joy Of Not Knowing It All* offers hope and opportunity. Ernie Zelinski inspires you to risk, be different, challenge the status quo, ruffle a few feathers, and in the process, truly make a big difference in this world.

This outstanding resource will help enhance the business performance of your staff and clients. Special prices apply for all organizations making premium purchases of 10 or more copies.

To order single copies on your credit card by telephone:

Call toll free 1-800-265-4559 in Canada and 1-800-356-9315 in the USA

The Joy Of Not Working

A Book For The Retired, Unemployed, and Overworked

The Joy Of Not Working has helped many individuals see hope and opportunity during retirement and layoffs where before they saw despair and dissatisfaction.

Blending humor, practical examples, numerous illustrations, and entertaining exercises, Ernie Zelinski has written a bestselling book which is humorous and easy to read. Because *The Joy Of Not Working* presents a serious and highly beneficial message on how to enjoy leisure like never before, career practitioners, outplacement consultants, and health counselors are recommending this book in life-style courses.

To order single copies on your credit card by telephone:

Call toll free 1-800-265-4559 in Canada and 1-800-356-9315 in the USA

To order <u>autographed</u> copies of ***The Joy Of Not Working*** by mail, send $19.95 per book postpaid (includes postage, handling, and tax). Send $14.95 per book postpaid (includes postage, handling, and tax) for orders of ten.

Visions International Publishing   Ph. (403) 436-1798
P.O. Box 4072
Edmonton, Alberta
Canada, T6E 4S8

Make cheques payable to Visions International Publishing

Name _____

Street_____

City _____ Province/State _____

Postal Or Zip Code _____